THE RIGHT WAY

Why the Left is wrong and the Right is "right"

By
Charles A. Salter

9/30/04

To Marty Young,

Happy birthday!

Charles A. Salter

PRESS

The Right Way
by Charles A. Salter

Printed in the United States of America

ISBN 1-594675-31-7

www.xulonpress.com

DEDICATION

T his book is dedicated to all the stalwart conservatives in our government who are trying to preserve the things that have made America great.

PREFACE

This book covers 30 topics which are crucial to the survival of America's freedom and classic way of life. They are in alphabetic order, which makes it easy to find whichever topic you are looking for. On the left hand page starts the liberal Left's view of that subject, while on the right side begins the conservative or right-wing view. Opposite philosophical positions are on opposing sides of the same opened page, to make all the clearer the distinctions between the two.

Yes, I know that not every left-wing person or self-identified liberal necessarily believes in all the left-wing views as I have described them...ditto for the other side of the aisle. Many people fall somewhere in the middle on virtually all issues, or accept the Left's view on some while the Right's view on others. I certainly don't claim that every liberal politician will necessarily push the left-wing outlook on all policy issues, or that self-identified conservatives will always vote for the conservative position.

Nevertheless, while any given individual may fall anywhere in between the opposite poles on these 30 positions, I think it is fair to say that generally, people who are most left-wing or liberal will tend towards the positions I describe as the Left's, and that generally, people who are most right-wing or conservative will tend towards the positions I describe as the right way.

You must decide for yourself which you think is the right way for America to go.

ABORTION

THE LEFT:
"A Woman's Right to Choose."
"Keep Your Hands Off My Body."
"Keep Abortion Safe and Legal."

So go the slogans on the left side of this debate. Before birth, the fetus is just a useless blob of tissue with no more legal standing than a wart or tumor. If the mother wants to get rid of it, that is no one else's business but hers. It doesn't matter what her parents or husband or boyfriend thinks or wants. Her ability to freely choose her reproductive destiny is paramount. Indeed, taxpayers must be forced to fund abortions for women who can't afford them—otherwise their ability to choose would be limited by economics. Similarly, medical schools must be forced to train doctors in abortion techniques and hospitals must be forced to permit abortions in their facilities. In short, any impediment to a woman's right to choose must be eliminated.

The Left believes the right wing must never be allowed to turn back the clock to a time when women who wanted abortions had to risk their lives in dirty back alleys to rid themselves of "the products of conception." In the 1973 Roe v. Wade decision the Supreme Court ruled once and for all that abortion is a "constitutional right."

Leftists who take their own propaganda seriously sometimes believe that the "miracle of birth" is that what was before a meaningless blob of cells somehow turns into an actual human baby only by being squeezed through the birth canal. Others take the extreme view that life at any point is really no more significant than non-life. Some radicals who pursue that line of thought actually maintain that, "A rock is a tree is a boy." In other words, everything visible in the universe, living or not living, plant or animal or human, is composed of the same kinds of atoms and molecules and none of it really has any deeper meaning or importance than simple chemistry, so you may as well do what you want.

Leftists who take this view to its logical conclusion believe the "right to choose" should extend to partial-birth abortion, where a live baby is almost completely born and then killed at the last moment. Others believe in infanticide, the idea that the parents should be free to kill their offspring well after birth if various kinds of physical or mental defects should appear.

THE RIGHT: Conservatives take seriously the view in the Declaration of Independence that the true function of government is to protect our rights to "life, liberty, and the pursuit of happiness." Thus we are concerned not only with the pregnant woman's rights, but also with those of the unborn child.

Despite left-wing propaganda to the contrary, the unborn baby is a not a part of the mother's body, but rather a genetically and biologically separate organism merely residing within it. At the moment of conception, the new life receives half its genes from the father and half from the mother. That first cell doesn't yet look like much, but it already has its own unique genetic composition. The cells rapidly grow, divide and specialize, so that within about three weeks there is a primitive heart that pumps blood in the tiny embryo. By about two months, about the time the woman may first realize she is pregnant, all the organs (brain, eyes, arms, legs, etc.) that distinguish this life as human have already begun to appear. A few months later, when many abortions take place, all the baby's senses are intact. It can respond to bright lights, to sound, to touch…and to pain. Psychologists have proved that fetuses near the end of pregnancy can even learn simple sensation-response connections while still within the womb.

There is no such thing as a "safe" abortion since killing the tiny human residing within her body is the whole point of the procedure. In a successful abortion, a human being is destroyed, usually in cruel and painful ways in which the baby gets no anesthetic at all. There are also risks to the mother. Many women have suffered physical consequences such as excessive bleeding, resulting infertility, or even occasionally death due to botched abortions. For many years afterwards, many women experience psychological and emotional consequences such as guilt and bitter regret. There is considerable evidence that having an abortion when young increases the woman's chances of getting breast cancer when older. Why? One theory is that pregnancy hormones have a powerful effect on breast tissue, and when the normal process is interrupted by abortion, tissue growth may continue into abnormal directions such as cancer.

Leftists pretend that they are "pro-choice," but they aren't for choice in general, but only for the pro-abortion choice. They are quite eager to forbid choice to medical schools, hospitals, and physicians who don't agree with them and who don't want to perform abortions. They don't care one whit about the freedom of choice for taxpayers who believe it is morally repellent to use their tax money for someone else's abortion.

The U.S. Supreme Court in the 1973 Roe v. Wade decision made a grave error in turning from the interpretation of the U.S. Constitution which actually exists to inventing new "rights" by legislating from the bench. (see also **JUDICIARY**). Humans have been "endowed by their Creator with certain unalienable Rights, that among these are life," to quote the Declaration of Independence, and no amount of word distortion by liberal judges can change eternal truths. There are better ways to help women dealing with unwanted pregnancies, e.g., adoption and crisis pregnancy centers to take care of their needs should they decide to keep their babies.

There are a few extremists who justify killing abortionists, but right-thinking conservatives clearly condemn the taking of life in the name of "pro-life."

AMENDMENT, FIRST

THE LEFT: Liberals love to claim that the First Amendment to the U.S. Constitution clearly mandates that we enforce a high wall of total separation between church and state. It is not only illegal but reprehensible if anyone in public refers to God or Jesus Christ in a respectful way (but as a curse it is okay). Therefore, we must take swift and punitive action to ensure that no one ever prays in school—they must not even be allowed a respectful "moment of silence" in the beginning of the school day, lest some backwards fundamentalist kid dare to silently think a brief prayer in the privacy of his own mind. No one may bring the Bible or other religious books to school or meet as a religious group on school property even after hours to privately discuss their ridiculous, old-fashioned beliefs.

Similarly, liberals want to ban words such as "Christmas" and speak instead of secular things such as "Winter Holiday" only. They won't allow Christmas carols that refer to the divine, though it is acceptable to sing about Rudolph the red-nosed reindeer and other purely non-religious holiday topics. No crèche scenes can be allowed in public anywhere, nor any other Judeo-Christian symbols such as the Ten Commandments.

It is paramount that nowhere in America is any public recognition given to the Judeo-Christian religions, even in areas where 99.99% of the residents are believers, lest some solitary agnostic, atheist, or member of another religion like Islam be offended. That's the American Way (at least according to "People for the American Way").

The Left thinks that the First Amendment goes on to ensure complete freedom to the press and all forms of personal expression, such as cursing in public, pornography, nudism, burning the American flag as a protest statement, etc. No one is allowed to censor such activities or even to withhold their tax money from supporting publicly-funded art that mocks or profanes religion, such as the infamous "crucifix in a jar of urine" art piece, or the portrait of Mary, the mother of Jesus, covered in dung. The only acceptable limits on freedom of speech are against prayer and God-talk in public. Even in churches themselves, it is not permissible to say non-politically correct things based on outmoded old religious myths, such as there being anything wrong with homosexuality.

As Karl Marx said, "Religion is the opiate of the people," and leftists feel it is time that they win this war on the "drug" of religion once and for all. As one letter to the editor put it when talking about a ban on gay marriage, "If we are going to ban anything, it should be the thing that has caused more war, more conflict, more atrocities, more heinous and brutal death, and more destruction to our world. Only when we ban religion will we have peace."

THE RIGHT: The real First Amendment to the U.S. Constitution bears almost no resemblance to what the Left now pretends. As with the entire document, they have twisted it over time into the antithesis of what it plainly says. Here are the actual words written by the Founding Fathers, words which have never been officially changed or revoked:

> "Congress shall make no law respecting an establishment of religion, or prohibiting the free exercise thereof; or abridging the freedom of speech, or the press, or the right of the people to peaceably assemble, and to petition the government for a redress of grievances."

There is not one word ANYWHERE in the U.S. Constitution about the supposed "separation of church and state." Thomas Jefferson did use the phrase in a private letter to the Danbury Baptists about 200 years ago, but that was not part of the Constitution, and he never meant it to exclude all vestiges of religion from public life, for he supported, for example, publicly funded chaplains. It has only been in about the last 50 years that leftists have successfully turned that phrase into a sledgehammer to stamp out all signs of religion in public.

The first clause does state that Congress cannot establish a single mandatory religion for the American people, the kind of official state-run church known in England at that time, for example. But that does not enshrine secularism as the official "religion" of the land, either, or deny to believers the right to express themselves in public. The very next clause makes clear that freedom of religious expression, anywhere and everywhere, is the law of the land. The Left has no right whatsoever to constantly censor religious expression in the schools or anywhere else. That they do so regardless of the constitutional facts speaks volumes about their irrational hostility towards religion and their totalitarian desire to impose their own beliefs on others.

The third clause does ensure our freedom of speech—clearly meaning verbal communication (as in conveying one's political or religious beliefs) but not absurd things like wanton pornography and artistic filth under the concept of freedom of "expression." Visible behavior and speech are not the same thing.

The fourth clause does indeed provide for freedom of the press, but the Left seems to like this only when it promotes left-wing causes. Watch them wail and scream if a newspaper or radio talk show promotes a right-wing view. Then they seek some excuse to shut them up. Similarly, they are for peaceful (or sometimes even violent) protests in support of the Left, e.g., the anti-war demonstrations and riots of the Viet Nam period. But they don't seem to appreciate that their opponents should also have the freedom to peacefully protest. For example, the media will always give great coverage to a demonstration by a tiny group of leftists, but will typically ignore or downplay a huge demonstration by a major group of conservatives (e.g., the prolife protests every year on the anniversary of the Roe v. Wade decision).

As far as banning religion, as many leftists burn with desire to do, how do they plan to accomplish that? Stalin, Hitler, Mao, and Pol Pot, among other vicious dictators of the last century, murdered tens of millions in their drive to suppress religion and did not succeed. While some zealots like Islamic terrorists have killed in the name of their religion, even greater mayhem has been caused by such totalitarian atheists trying to destroy religion and enslave a populace.

AMENDMENT, SECOND—See **GUN CONTROL**

AMERICA

THE LEFT: If ever there was a country deserving scorn, it is America. It was founded in bloodshed and treachery, wiping out the Indian tribes who lived here in peace and harmony with nature. Its government was birthed in bloodshed, the illegitimate war with England in the 1770's, and the society built itself up by the blood of countless slaves. It has scarcely had a year of peace since its founding, since it is imperialistically trying to enforce its will on other nations all over the world, stirring up strife everywhere it goes.

It is a sexist, racist, imperialistic, homophobic, and worthless culture. It is deserving only of contempt and condemnation. It is a wasteful nation which exploits the world, selfishly using up 60% of the world's resources. At the time of the 9/11 terrorist attacks some leftists even in the U.S. ranted that America finally got a taste of what it deserved. Said history professor Richard Berthold to his University of New Mexico class, "anyone who can blow up the Pentagon has my vote."

And regarding the 2003 invasion of Iraq, Nicholas DeGenova, an assistant professor at Columbia (NY) University said at a campus teach-in, "U.S. patriotism is inseparable from imperial warfare and white supremacy...The only true heroes are those who find ways that help defeat the U.S. military." He also wished a "million Mogadishus" on the U.S., referring to the "Blackhawk Down" incident in Somalia in 1993 where 19 U.S. servicemen were slaughtered in an ambush.

America should never be allowed to act on its own, according to the Left, for its jingoistic nature will always choose wrong. If anything bad happens anywhere in the world, it is probably America's fault. Therefore, America must be made subject to the U.N. where the oppressed peoples of third world countries can finally break America's stranglehold on the globe. Ideally, there will be revolution in America to overthrow its warmongering capitalistic ways and bring about a new People's Republic.

The whole idea of separate nations is anachronistic anyway. The Left's ultimate goal is to do away with America entirely and have it merge with the rest of the world into a one-world government, of which the U.N. is but the beginning. Only then can the world finally know peace.

Conservatives who think America is something special or great are misguided fools or worse, according to the Left. As Samuel Johnson said, "Patriotism is the last refuge of scoundrels." Conservatives with their extremist agenda have no place in legitimate mainstream politics and should be made to feel like the outcasts they really are. They will have no place at all in the coming one-world society, unless perhaps they allow themselves to be re-educated into politically correct thought.

THE RIGHT: If ever there was a country deserving praise and respect, it is the United States of America. While no country has ever been perfect, America is one of the very few which have even tried to establish and live up to godly ideals. In a world of countless brutal tyrannies, America stands for democracy and freedom. Where other regimes rule with iron-fisted terror, America governs with the freely given consent of the governed. While other nations seek war to enlarge their territories and possessions, America seeks peace whenever possible, and only resorts to war when it believes the war "just," one in which a greater good can be achieved only at the terrible cost of war. Even when forced to fight, America does so to liberate, not to conquer. To bring aid and comfort, not oppression.

The idea that almost any other culture is superior to America's is a ridiculous, unrealistic, left-wing fantasy. To which country do the oppressed peoples of the world always turn? When they vote with their feet by leaving behind everything to immigrate to a new country, to which one do they most want to go? Even the leftists who so praise the communist system of Cuba or mainland China, interestingly, don't choose to immigrate there. Such leftists are hypocrites, professing to believe in the political equivalent of Santa Claus or the Easter Bunny, but almost never choosing actually to live in those cultures they so highly applaud. Even as they bitterly condemn everything about America, they paradoxically have enough common sense still to live here, in a culture where they have the freedom to spout such nonsense without ending up in prison or a torture chamber as they would if they became citizens of China or Cuba or Saddam Hussein's Iraq and criticized those governments.

Ronald Reagan, one of America's best presidents ever, one who rolled back tyrannies and expanded freedom around the globe, put it best, likening America to a shining city on a hill:

" ...After 200 years, two centuries, she still stands strong and true on the granite ridge, and her glow has held steady no matter what storm. And she's still a beacon, still a magnet for all who must have freedom, for all the pilgrims from all the lost places who are hurtling through the darkness, toward home."

In a world that seems to turn inexorably toward chaos or tyranny, America offers the last best hope for freedom. Patriots who believe in reality rather than left-wing doggerel will support America with their dying breath so as to pass its bright light of freedom on to their children and grandchildren. As Wendell Phillips, the 19th century orator and columnist said, "Eternal vigilance is the price of liberty."

BILL OF RIGHTS—See **CONSTITUTION, U.S.**

CAPITAL PUNISHMENT

THE LEFT: The government should never set a bad example by killing anyone. According to liberals, execution as a punishment for crime is abhorrent for several reasons:

First, killing just begets a cycle of violence and encourages more violence in society. There is no way that capital punishment can act as a deterrent to suppress the violent crime rate.

Second, it is better to rehabilitate a criminal than to execute him. For even the worst, most sadistic mass murderers, life imprisonment with no possibility of parole is enough punishment to protect society from their further predations.

Third, it would be wrong to kill someone when there is a possibility of mistaken conviction. As one legal scholar put it, "Better to let a thousand criminals go free than imprison an innocent man." If later evidence proves innocence, we can always release an imprisoned person, but we can't bring him back to life after execution.

Finally, and most importantly, no murderer is really guilty anyway. It is always society's fault. If we eliminated poverty through the redistribution of income, raised kids well with good day care, and made sure people were kept occupied through such things as midnight basketball leagues in the inner city, then society would become perfect and crime would disappear.

THE RIGHT: As is so often the case, the Left Way sounds compassionate and nice on the surface. Certainly all of us can understand feeling squeamish about capital punishment and can barely imagine someone having to "pull the switch," so to speak. So if we are going to dwell on the plane of emotion only, the Left is probably going to win this argument.

But instead, let's dig into the facts and apply a little logic. When you examine this issue in the cold light of reality, it is easy to demolish the Left's arguments.

First, let's examine the issues of deterrence and protecting society. When looking at broad statistical studies, it is possible to find some which suggest that capital punishment seems to deter and other studies which suggest the opposite. But what is indisputable is that murderers who are executed can no longer commit crimes in this world, while those merely imprisoned can. Execution leads with absolute certainty to deterrence of further crimes by those who are put to death. Until fairly recently, it was not uncommon for murderers who were released from prison on parole, before their sentences were even fully served, to go out and kill again. To prevent this, we more often see these days calls to have a murderer given a life sentence "with no possibility of parole." Does that really solve the problem? No—how about the possibility of escape or future changes in the law (e.g., pardons by governors) or of hideous crimes of violence perpetrated while incarcerated? A live murderer can still commit crimes against guards and other prisoners in prison, but a dead one can't. And isn't it a strange paradox that the Left is so concerned about sparing the life of a criminal, no matter how fiendish, but has no problem with killing over a million innocent unborn babies every year (often in cruel and painful ways) in America alone?

Second, while no one wants to see an innocent person wrongfully convicted, does it really make sense to weight all of our courtroom rules towards letting a thousand guilty go free to avoid punishing one innocent person? If even 30% of the 1000 wrongfully released guilty go out and commit further crimes, then that is 300 more criminals on the loose and preying on the innocent in society. With the left wing approach, we thus spare one innocent but allow 300 or more other innocents to suffer. With the right approach, maybe we do occasionally let one suffer, but we spare the 300. And have there ever been any innocents wrongfully convicted and executed in modern America? Has the Left ever put forth a list of actual such cases, as contrasted with merely bleating about the hypothetical possibility of one?

The idea that individuals are never guilty (in the philosophical sense) for their own actions but that rather society is always at fault for crime is perhaps the biggest idiocy of all. What is society made of if not a collection of individuals? The Left believes people are innately good and perfect until corrupted by society, while the Right recognizes that all people are morally flawed and prone to do wrong things for selfish reasons (referred to as "original sin" in some circles). Please see the **CRIME & PUNISHMENT** entry for more discussion of this topic.

CIVIL RIGHTS

THE LEFT: Radicals believe that racism is absolutely endemic, staining every single thread of the fabric of society. White people have always been such racists that all of them should collectively feel ashamed for all the racist sins of the past. Even white people who have never engaged in overt racist acts or spoken openly a racist word in their entire lives, can safely be assumed probably to be racists in their hearts. The only way to prove otherwise is to immediately accede to all demands of any civil rights leader in America or they will betray themselves as closet racists still. It is impossible for whites not to be racist unless they devote themselves consciously and wholeheartedly to supporting all civil rights causes. Otherwise, they are beneficiaries of racism even if they don't practice it themselves.

To help atone for the sins of the past, liberals believe that whites today must eagerly embrace every sort of affirmative action program. In other words, because their great-great-great-grandparents might have benefited from slavery or other forms of racism 150 years ago, they should now recompense African Americans by gladly taking a back seat on the bus and freely allowing today's minorities to enjoy special advantages in the marketplace. For instance, minorities should be admitted into colleges and professional schools even if their SAT scores and grades are far below those of many whites who are rejected. After all, it's only because of racism that minorities get lower scores and grades. Similarly, desirable jobs should go to minorities even who are far less "qualified" in the traditional sense than white applicants. After all, it's only because of racism that they have fewer qualifications. Moreover, the nation as a whole should apologize for the slavery which ended in the 1860's and should now pay cash reparations to all African Americans, even those who are not descendants of long-ago slaves.

In other words, the Left believes that two wrongs make a right. Even today's whites who have never engaged in racist acts in their lives can pay for their forebears' sins by giving special privileges, apologies, and reparations to today's minorities, even those who have never suffered overt discrimination in their entire careers. It's collective, group rights which are important, not individual ones. Otherwise we'll never achieve inter-generational justice.

THE RIGHT: Two wrongs don't make a right, most particularly when the people being wronged now are innocent of doing the wrong before.

People today should not be punished for what others did centuries ago. If we are going to try to compensate for all the sins of the past, then everyone today will be both guilty by group association and an un-wronged beneficiary. Did some whites centuries ago enslave blacks? Absolutely. Did some blacks centuries ago enslave other blacks? Unquestionably. Haven't white people also been slaves in various past cultures? Of course! Do some people of all colors even today practice slavery? Unfortunately, yes.

This whole idea of collective guilt leads ultimately to all sorts of incredibly complex and paradoxical situations. Under most planned schemes of reparations, even whites today whose forbears sacrificed their lives fighting to end slavery would have to pay African Americans whose forbears were never slaves or even made and kept slaves themselves. That's not social justice; it's social idiocy!

And why do civil rights leaders today still obsess over American slavery, which ended in the 1860's, but don't seem to care about slavery going on now in other countries? For example, in Sudan today, black Muslims are enslaving (and committing other atrocities against) black Christians and pagans. The American Anti-Slavery Group (AASG) reports an alarming amount of slavery in many countries today (see the website http://www.iabolish.com for details on the millions of people enslaved around the world and how you can help). A current problem like that is something we can all actually do something about. Yet civil rights leaders are strangely silent.

Why do so many civil rights leaders complain so much about even the mildest forms of private, attitudinal racism on the part of whites, but have nothing to say about actual genocide against blacks in other countries? In Africa, for example, there have been cases of one tribe of blacks savagely slaughtering another tribe. For instance, in Rwanda in 1994, the Hutu tribe sadistically butchered some half million or more of the Tutsi tribe, often hacking them to pieces with machetes. Yet civil rights leaders again remained oddly silent. It appears they are much more concerned about minor indiscretions, if made by whites, than they are about incredibly gross mayhem, if done by blacks. And this silence about other countries is not a matter of reticence to interfere abroad. Liberals were very active for years in censuring South Africa for apartheid...until it was eliminated.

And what about reverse racism? The idea that whites are somehow uniquely racist is total nonsense. Are some whites racist? Certainly, but not all. Some African Americans are also racist, as are some Asians, some Indians, and some of any other group you can name. All cultures, ethnic groups, and other divisions of humanity harbor some racists. No individual anywhere is morally perfect. "For all have sinned and fallen short..."

Instead of continuing to decry long past problems which were already corrected ages ago through the Civil War and the abolition of slavery in America, let's focus on today's injustices that we can actually do something about. Instead of fretting over group rights and special privileges for some, why not do what the U.S. Constitution actually says and treat all individuals as equal under the law? Isn't that what Martin Luther King preached?

CLASS WARFARE

THE LEFT: As Karl Marx taught, society is divided up into social classes, and the desires of each are inevitably in conflict with the others. The rich upper class owns the means of production and selfishly seeks more and more gain for itself, which it typically does by exploiting the lower classes and the workers. In other words, owners get richer by taking most of the fruit of labor for themselves, while giving laborers the lowest possible wages and the worst working conditions they can get away with.

Other than outright revolution, the Left sees only two ways by which workers can improve their position. One is by uniting, as in forming labor unions, for in numbers there is some strength to counter the economic and political clout of the ruling class. The unions can then hold out for better wages and working conditions and go on strike if their demands are not sufficiently met. Ordinary union members must be kept on a tight leash, whether they wish to be or not, because a united front against management is essential.

The second recourse for the lower classes is government. A strong central government can force the upper class to do the right thing. The lower classes will naturally look to government as their savior. And herein lies a marvelous political opportunity for liberals: It is relatively easy for leftists to drum up voters and support for their parties and causes by promising a "free lunch," i.e., taking something from "the rich" and giving it to "the poor." Left wing politicians foment class strife and almost invariably cast economic issues in terms of class warfare because that way they can secure more votes, often enough to keep themselves in power.

For instance, if the right wing wants to cut taxes, thus allowing earners to keep more of what they have earned, leftists will condemn this as "giving tax cuts to the rich." They will complain that the lower class doesn't get "its fair share" of the federal tax largesse, somehow overlooking the fact that lower income earners get less back only because they put less in to begin with.

And if the conservatives fail to go along with any left-wing proposal for some new federal entitlement program or other benefit for lower income classes, the liberals will stridently denounce right-wingers as being "against the poor," "only for the rich," or heartlessly wanting to let the poor starve or be cast into the streets. As Howard Dean, one of the Democratic candidates for President in 2004 put it, for instance, "The tax cuts are designed to destroy Social Security, Medicare, our public schools and our public services through starvation and privatization." Note the imputation of intent. He does not simply imply that the tax cuts might incidentally harm these other government activities; he asserts that they are explicitly designed to do so.

Leftists never tire of the class warfare gambit because it works politically for them time and again. It is one of the most formidable weapons in their arsenal.

THE RIGHT: Class warfare works so well politically because there is a grain of truth to it, and the erroneous aspects can usually be glossed over with the help of willing media accomplices. In the late 19th century and early 20th century there were so-called "robber barons" who believed in building up their own estates at the expense of others. They charged customers for their products as much as they could while simultaneously paying their laborers as little as possible. That is abhorrent and wrong. Tendencies toward such selfishness at the expense of others are inherent in the human condition and crop up today as well. But selfishness is not just a moral flaw of "the rich."

The purveyors of class warfare overlook the selfishness of the other groups in this class warfare scenario. Leftists openly appeal to cold, naked envy when they promise to take from people who earned something and then give it to "the poor" who did nothing to earn it. They seem to forget that envy is one of the classic seven deadly sins. And they completely overlook their own selfishness and greed in trying to buy political power with money that is not theirs, taking what they want from others with no thought to the consequences. They are themselves a type of political "robber baron," no more moral or compassionate (despite all their hollow claims to such) than the robber barons of old. As is often said, those who want to rob Peter to pay Paul can usually count on Paul's political support. But it is still a type of stealing, even if the government is the agent of this "robbery."

Casting all capitalists and managers today in the image of robber barons is ludicrous and offensive, and totally overlooks the reality of enlightened management in most businesses today. For instance, trained and productive American workers now have it pretty good for the most part, with adequate income in most jobs and all sorts of benefits such as a limited number of work hours per week, medical and dental insurance, paid vacations, pension plans, and even increasingly co-ownership in the company (through stock ownership). No, the situation is not perfect for everyone, and unskilled laborers at the bottom of the scale do often struggle financially. The key problem there typically is that their efforts don't produce enough value to the company so it can afford higher pay. For instance, a burger joint can't pay a burger flipper $15 an hour if his efforts produce only $10 of net income per hour for the company. Such workers do need help, but class warfare is not the answer.

Class warfare leftists also overlook the great harm which results from their policies when enacted. If you take more and more money away from the people who actually earn it, eventually many of them will start working less or quit altogether (e.g., early retirement or leaving the country). And raising up a huge dependent underclass which expects only to receive and receive without having to contribute anything in return creates only disaster, an increase in all sorts of social pathologies such as broken families, alcoholism, and crime.

For more on this subject see **POVERTY**.

COMMUNISM—See **SOCIALISM**

CONSTITUTION, U.S.

THE LEFT: Liberals believe that the U.S. Constitution can no longer be interpreted by federal judges in the way that stodgy old Founding Fathers of centuries ago intended. It is ridiculous to be tied to the distant past. Instead, they consider the Constitution a "living document" meant to evolve continually to match changes in the nature of society and its needs. Only elite, open-minded, left-leaning jurists can be trusted to make these revolutionary adaptations, however.

Thus, for example, when there was a growing controversy over the morality of abortion in the 1960's and 1970's, there was no need to depend on the will of the majority of the public or to bother the elected executive and legislative branches to gradually work things out through the tedious and uncertain law-making process. Instead, courageous left-leaning Supreme Court justices could jump in and immediately resolve the crisis by suddenly in 1973 (Roe v. Wade) finding never-before-noticed provisions in the Constitution that provided for a "constitutional right" for abortion related to an also never-before-seen provision for a right to privacy in reproductive issues.

Similarly, state supreme courts could employ this elasticity concept toward the law by stretching state constitutions to match their pre-conceived notions about what the law should be. Thus the Massachusetts Supreme Court in 2003 could suddenly find a right to gay marriage in the Massachusetts Constitution, something heretofore unnoticed and unseen by generations of previous lawmakers and jurists.

Considering the law completely malleable in the hands of left-leaning justices is a magical way to cut the Gordian knots which sometimes tie up society. Presto! The enlightened judges cut right through the knot of red tape and enforce their will on a society, whether it wants it or not.

The Left is terrified that this complete and total freedom of judges to impose their will on the people might slip away or be preempted by extremist right-wing judges. Therefore it is essential that the Left destroy such a judge by any means possible and fight to the bitter end to keep such a jurist from being appointed to the higher courts. Thus was Judge Bork prevented from reaching the Supreme Court and Clarence Thomas nearly was. So-called strict constitutional constructionists, judges who stick to interpreting the law as it is actually written, are the number one impediment to the left-wing agenda. All means of preventing them from reaching higher courts are justified, even bottling up their nominations in committee or filibustering, refusing to let them face an open vote in the Senate where they might perchance be confirmed. This is one situation where the end clearly justifies the means, no matter how underhanded.

THE RIGHT: The actual U.S. Constitution carefully crafted by America's Founding Fathers was explicitly intended to prevent the reappearance of tyranny by separating the powers of government into three different branches—the executive (the President and his staff), the legislative (the Senate and House of Representatives in Congress), and the judicial The third branch was meant to be weaker than the other two, since those branches were directly accountable to the people through periodic elections while the federal judiciary wasn't. Therefore, the judicial branch was specifically limited to interpreting the law, not making it. Only the legislative branch could actually produce new laws.

Many of the Founding Fathers were hesitant to sign the Constitution as it was first proposed because they feared that future leaders would usurp their constitutional limitations and assume too much power. They realized the truth of the dictum we now know simply as "power corrupts, and absolute power corrupts absolutely." With power spread among three branches, the hope was that if any one tried to assume illegitimate power that the other two could bring it back into line. Moreover, they added ten amendments to the original document, the so-called "Bill of Rights" to explicitly specify where the government would always be limited in restricting freedom of the people. Even though some signers believed the basic document implied all those rights already, others would not sign until they were explicit. Yet the Left is constantly chipping away even at these explicit rights, particularly the freedom of religion (see **AMENDMENT, FIRST**) and gun rights in the Second Amendment (see **GUN CONTROL**).

The Founding Fathers realized, of course, that future changes in society might require adaptations to the Constitution, so produced a specific process for making such changes through amendments, a process the Left scorns because it slows the implementation of their agenda.

All federal officers, not only the top leaders of government but even all members of the military, when sworn into office pledge to "defend the Constitution from all enemies, foreign and domestic." Left wing jurists who in effect legislate from the bench have violated that oath and become the very enemies we should defend against. When they substitute their own preferences for what the law clearly states, short-circuiting the proper amendment process, they become the very kind of tyrants that our system was intended to protect us from. It is way past time for the executive and legislative branches to step in and restore the balance of powers. We need something like a constitutional amendment making it simple for the Congress to impeach an out-of-control judge. If that happened a few times, maybe more judges would stick to following their sworn oaths of office.

An elastic, "living" constitution ever changing by the whims of judges protects no one. Even the most ardent left-wing supporters of judicial activism would clearly see the point if the Supreme Court were ever to gore one of their choice oxen for a change. Imagine the outcry if an arrogant Court began to squelch the freedom of the press as it has the freedom of religion, or if it declared it legal to kill abortionists as it has to kill unborn babies, or some other equally outlandish departure from normality and tradition. What we so desperately need are strict-constructionist judges who will intepret the true Constitution as it is actually written, thus protecting all of us, left and right and middle-roaders alike. See also **JUDICIARY**.

CRIME AND PUNISHMENT

THE LEFT: Liberals believe every person is born good and decent and innocent in every respect. They only do something we don't approve of if forced into it by society, if the circumstances of their lives compel them in that direction.

Therefore, if someone breaks the law we don't look internally to their character for the reason, but rather externally to society at large. We know it can't come from within, therefore it MUST come from without. We'll look for the causes of crime in poverty, inadequate education, too much unstructured time on their hands, and racism, etc.

Liberals consider the perpetrators of crime as victims, perhaps even more so as victims than those suffering the acts of crime. After all, the so-called "victims of crime" are often part of the societal structure which caused the criminal to break the law. They are at least partly responsible, in some cases largely responsible, for the criminal behavior. The so-called "criminals" themselves are not responsible at all; they are the real victims here of the entire system. For instance, poverty causes crime, so it is not the "criminal's" fault that he resents the rich and steals from them. But the rich man from whom he steals IS at fault for perpetrating the system of inequality that leads to poverty and racism and makes the real victim here resort to criminal acts.

Since the criminal is never responsible and never at fault and is actually the victim of the system, then any form of punishment is completely inappropriate and will only prolong or worsen the cycle of violence or other criminal behavior. We should hold an enlightened view of compassion for the so-called criminal and seek to rehabilitate—not punish or otherwise harm—him. Liberals therefore instruct conservatives that their lust for vengeance is counterproductive at best, and at worst reflects a mean-spiritedness that is itself one of the leading societal causes of crime. They say society should see the criminal as the injured party, not as the person responsible. We should pity him, not hate or fear him. We should seek to help him, not punish him.

Here is a perfect illustration of right-wing folly, according to the Left: The prison system and its population have been expanding for years. We now have approximately two million people behind bars in America. Yet crime has been dropping recently; so why should we keep imprisoning more and more people?

THE RIGHT: As with so many issues, the Left has everything exactly backwards. And this is not just a matter of being wrong in the philosophical sense, with regard to winning an abstract debate. Quite the contrary—the Left's corruption of the entire criminal justice system over a couple of generations has had serious real life effects, dramatically increasing crime of all sorts throughout all areas of society, at least until people wised up and stopped listening to them. Implementation of the Left's philosophy for decades led to real people just like you, like your parents or children, real people being mugged and raped and killed.

When you turn dark into light and light into dark, when you make criminals into victims and crime victims into the bad guys, when you reward bad behavior and punish good, you get more bad and less good.

Despite the fond fantasies of the Left, people are born not perfect, but with profound moral flaws. Some people seek God and choose consistently to strive to better themselves and, despite occasional mistakes, become generally solid and productive citizens. It is well known that even in prison populations, involvement with a genuinely Christian prison ministry or para-church group can help dramatically to transform lives through the infusion of spiritual power. But some people don't even bother to try to improve their characters but rather gladly wallow in crime and chalk up an increasingly evil and repulsive rap sheet of criminal acts. It's got nothing to do with poverty and all the other tired left-wing excuses, but rather character. You can be poor but honest, or wealthy but crooked.

Many Americans alive today can remember a more innocent time in American society when it was safe to leave one's home or car unlocked or to let younger children play at will throughout the neighborhood. But then the Left turned everything upside down, and decent people in effect imprisoned themselves behind high walls, burglar bars, and guarded gates, while the criminals roamed freely, and even if they were caught they openly mocked the system because they knew nothing would really be done to them. But then more and more Americans began to wake up to the truth and insist that their elected officials do something about the guilty to protect the innocent (a novel concept to the Left). For instance, New York City was a veritable playground for criminals for some time, until a new mayor rode into town after a successful career as a tough federal prosecutor. Rudolph Guiliani decided to crack down on crime...much to the horror of the city's liberals. But strict law enforcement worked, crime dropped, and ordinary people could breathe freer in New York.

Similarly, Virginia and other states began to impose strict mandatory sentences for crimes using guns (mandatory so liberal judges couldn't let the criminals go free) and saw a dramatic decrease in crime. "Three strikes and you're out" and other tough laws have done much to reduce crime, again by limiting the freedom of liberal judges to set criminals loose. Punishment works because it makes criminal behavior less attractive and rewarding. Leftists claim to be perplexed that as crime continues to fall that we keep locking up record numbers of people. They are so blind that it is almost funny. Crime is more under control today precisely because we have been strict about locking up criminals. Isn't it obvious?

DRUG USE

THE LEFT: "Tune in. Turn on. Drop out."

That was one of the popular slogans among the 60's radicals, many of whom now are leaders in the liberal establishment. It meant to open your mind to the left-wing wavelength, to alter your consciousness with drugs, and to abandon the conservative mainstream society with its absurd middle class values such as high goals, hard work, achievement, and sexual fidelity.

Instead, one of the chief radical values became, "If it feels good, do it!" Take no thought to the future or to responsibilities for others in the present. Instead, get high, take it easy, and do what you want. "Me first" is all that counts.

The infamous late drug guru Timothy Leary, formerly a professor at Harvard University, taught that drugs could not only relax you and make you feel good, but could expand your consciousness and even enhance your spirituality, putting yourself more in touch with "god" (apparently not the personal "I AM" God of the Bible, but rather an amorphous, vaguely mystical, impersonal force of the universe). Leary, as well as other drug gurus, used to travel from college campus to campus, preaching the "good news" of the power of drugs to eager throngs who delighted over every word. Here was an expert, a scientist, confirming what they most wanted to believe, namely that the easy path of drugs and bed was not only fun, but actually enlightening.

Some movies of the period, such as the cult favorite EASY RIDER, celebrated a life centered almost entirely on acquiring drugs, selling drugs, and enjoying drugs, occasionally along with a little sex. Such movies portrayed conservatives as vicious and evil, willing to do violence against or even kill fun-loving hippies out of sheer spite.

Things may not be quite as flagrant and open currently as in the radical 60's. But drug use and the approval of illegal drugs is still very much a part of left-wing life. It would be hard to imagine a Hollywood party or New York gala frequented by the liberal elite without freely available drugs such as cocaine, marijuana, or ecstasy. To many left-wing people, "having a joint" together is just as natural as sharing tea or coffee is to conservatives.

THE RIGHT: All drugs, both legal medicines and illegal recreational chemicals, carry a certain risk, and the wise conservative will be discerning about putting any such chemicals into his or her body. Anyone who doubts the potency of even normal medicines need only look at the warning insert in the package for typically a long list of side effects and other hazards. For a complete description of the risks of any particular drug, even the humble and common aspirin, consult the PHYSICIAN'S DESK REFERENCE (or PDR in medical-speak). This is essentially an encyclopedia on current medications, describing for each its chemical nature, how it works, its risks and benefits.

To say that all medicines carry risk does not imply that they shouldn't be used. To the contrary, when a physician prescribes one, the whole point is that he believes the potential benefits outweigh the risks. Some medications are the only thing keeping certain people alive. For instance, patients with extremely high blood pressure, severe diabetes, or serious infections need their pills or injections or they may die. Of course, when taking a prescription or over-the-counter medication, it is important to follow the directions, take no more than necessary, and to note side effects, reporting them to one's doctor if they are serious.

Now, apply that same kind of discernment to illegal recreational drugs. There is no real benefit and there are whopping risks. A person may desire to "get high" and consider that a type of psychological benefit, but we are talking here about objective medical benefits (e.g., comparable to insulin keeping a diabetic alive). Other than possibly pain relief in terminal cases, there are NO such benefits from the harder drugs such as cocaine, LSD, PCP, and heroin (the jury is still out on marijuana's impact on glaucoma and cancer symptoms). The risks are incalculably greater than for ordinary medications, including the possibility of being arrested and jailed for breaking the law, the substandard purity of the compounds (meaning the presence of contaminants, which may be toxic), the unknown strength of the drug (which may lead to overdose), and the very real risk of death after even one dose. Some liberals say, "Well, how do you know you don't like it if you don't try it? Just try it once." The basketball player Len Bias, who had just signed a lucrative contract with the pros, went out to celebrate, had cocaine for the first time in his life, and promptly died. Deaths due to illegal drugs are not at all uncommon, and the list of celebrities dying from them continues to grow—think Janis Joplin and Jimi Hendrix from the 1960's all the way up to John Belushi in the 1980's and River Phoenix more recently.

The cost is not only to the victim who suffers directly from the drug, but the uncountable toll to society of drug lords and dealers corrupting the system, torturing and killing people in their way, and users committing crimes to raise the money to buy the drugs.

People on the right generally agree that illegal drugs are not a good thing and that people shouldn't take them. Beyond that, however, there are differences of opinion. Some believe in tough anti-drug laws and strict enforcement. Others take a more libertarian view that legalization would get the criminals out of the drug business, allow easier identification and treatment of users, and give citizens more freedom to make their own choices. Most conservatives tend to favor the get-tough approach, but some leading conservatives disagree.

EDUCATION

THE LEFT: Liberals see the public education system as the best way the Left has to break the influence conservative, middle-class parents have on their children and to remold young minds for the brave new world. Since they can't change everyone in the old generation, the Left wants total control over the education system so they can shape the next generation to their liking. This way, they will ultimately win all the marbles because in the future they will own the majority and its votes.

Therefore, the Left holds these positions related to public education:

- Parents should have little or no say over their children's education. The less parents know about what is going on, the better. Parents should not be aware how their own old-fashioned values and beliefs are being trampled on in their children's reshaping in school.

- It is far more important to teach left-wing values and attitudes in school than to teach children basic fundamentals of learning (reading and writing, etc.) and how to think for themselves. For instance, it is important to have kids distrust the America of old and the America their parents knew, so history will be rewritten to make America the bane of the world, rotten to the core, and multi-culturalism will spread the message that all other systems are better, and civics requirements will be eliminated altogether so that children won't learn about the true nature of their Constitution and how government is supposed to be run.

- Ridiculous, out-moded morality must be erased and the "new morality" instilled. Therefore, a huge proportion of school time will be devoted to sex education and instruction, teaching that "gay is okay," that it is fine to experiment with sex, and that teen pregnancies should be

44

eliminated by abortion without the knowledge or consent of the girl's parents.

- To foster all these departures from morality and the past and to instill in children a total faith in the Left, it is essential that all references to the Judeo-Christian God must be utterly eradicated. Eastern religions, American Indian mysticism, witchcraft, and other pagan traditions are okay, because they make no demands for spiritual allegiance and commitment to morality. But Christianity has got to be completely eliminated. It is the one and only force that the Left can't face in open battle, so it must be subverted.

- Home schooling is very, very bad and must be fought politically in every way possible because home-schooled kids are largely beyond the reach of the Left (except through the media) and will become part of an active right-wing remnant in the next generation—a minority, but still a formidable force to be reckoned with in the next generation that will slow the Left's ultimate victory. Better to defeat them now and force them into the fold while they are still malleable. The same thing holds true for private religious education and vouchers for educational choice. Anything that helps remove kids from the Left's influence or control must be opposed.

THE RIGHT: Education used to be considered a gift of God and was promulgated by churches and churchmen. In religious private schooling, that is still the case. But once the government took over the role of education and made it "public," it was just a matter of time before it became more and more secular.

Most on the right could accept secular education if it remained truly neutral on religious matters (as opposed to openly and hopelessly hostile) and if high educational standards were maintained. But the masters of left-wing education care little if anything about actual education as the word was understood for hundreds of years, namely, the mastery of the basics arts and sciences and learning how to reason and think for oneself. The Left seems intent rather on brainwashing, creating blind followers, in political, religious, and moral matters about which they are totally unqualified in the sense that they base everything on a false foundation (secular humanism) rather than reality. As usual, they have everything exactly backwards.

- Parents should be intimately involved in all aspects of their children's education. True, some parents are negligent in this area, but the school system should encourage more involvement, not try to avoid it.

- Education should focus almost entirely on the fundamentals such as reading, writing, mathematics, history, and the ability to reason. There should be nothing on trying to instill the so-called "new morality" which is just the old pagan immorality with a "new and improved" name to garner more acceptance. Schools should play a role in instilling values, but these should be traditional values as held by the parents, not countercultural values that attack everything the parents believe in. This is particularly true with respect to sexual morality—the schools have no business contradicting thousands of years of biblical teaching and brainwashing kids to think that homosexuality, premarital sex, and abortions are all wonderful and perfectly acceptable, normal things without any unpleasant consequences.

- For the schools to expel God and all things godly is the biggest travesty of all. The vast majority of parents believe in God, as do many of the students, but they are scorned or even punished if they dare to pray in school (even privately, over lunch) or meet as a prayer group on school grounds after school is over, etc. The left-wing high priests of "tolerance" are the least tolerant people in all of society, if you dare disagree with their complete censorship of God.

- A generation or two ago, there was little home-schooling because there was little need of it. Schools reflected and fostered the values of the community rather than trampling on them. There has been a huge percent increase in home schooling as public schools have declined, and on average, home schooled children way outperform the products of a plummeting public school system. Liberals generally blame any school problems or failures on the lack of sufficient tax money, but in constant dollars more is spent now per student than 50 years ago, but the product is far, far worse. Money itself is not the answer. To restore the schools we need accountability to parents and taxpayers, a restoration of traditional values, and a focus on genuine educational skills rather than left-wing dogma.

EUTHANASIA

THE LEFT: Everyone should have the right to die with dignity. This means each person should freely be able to choose the timing and manner of his own death. Suicide should not be illegal, it should be applauded. If a hospital patient, for example, is bedridden in a terminal condition from which he will never recover, his quality of life is so impaired that he would be better off dead. Family members as well as medical staff must respect the patient's wishes and provide him the means to terminate his life when he is ready.

Dr. Kevorkian, the so-called "Dr. Death," is to be applauded for standing up to the unjust laws which prevent either passive euthanasia (allowing a patient to die rather than continue trying to save him medically) or active euthanasia (deliberately taking his life, as through the administration of a fatal dose of drugs). Dr. Kevorkian is a pioneer, a great hero to the Left, for defying legal restrictions and direct court orders by giving ill patients the means to terminate their own lives.

The Hemlock Society (so-named for the botanical drug by which the Greek philosopher Socrates took his own life) is also to be applauded for pushing to legalize suicide and make the means of suicide available to all.

The Left also sees a great value to society of euthanasia. It is well known that most of one's medical expenses are incurred in the last year or two of life, when one is fighting terminal disease. Euthanasia can not merely help the patient avoid all that terminal decline and suffering, but can save society untold billions in medical bills, nursing home expenses, etc. Plus, the surviving family members don't have to endure watching their relative's slow, painful decline, nor do they have to care for relatives who are totally out of it, like Alzheimer's patients, for example, who gradually descend into total dementia. People like that, who are demented, or severely brain damaged, or in a coma are unable to make the sensible decision for euthanasia on their own, so that decision should be made for them. As Dr. Peter Singer, professor of bioethics at Princeton University has declared, *"Once the religious mumbo-jumbo surrounding the term "human" has been stripped away... we will not regard as sacrosanct the life of each and every member of our species."*

Who can make that decision? Family members, if they are willing to decide sensibly. If they are not, then wise doctors on the case should be allowed to make it. If the doctors are not courageous enough to make the proper left-wing choice, then the courts or a new government agency will be empowered to do so. According to the Left, no one has the right to continue suffering indefinitely at society's expense.

THE RIGHT: As the description of the Left's point of view should illustrate, arguments for euthanasia start on a slippery slope from letting the patient take his own life if he wishes, but slide quickly to a position where the patient's life will be taken even when he doesn't want to die. Deliberately killing a patient who wishes to continue living currently goes by another name—premeditated murder—but you can count on that to change as the left-wing view becomes ascendant in society. It will be called something like "compassionate termination of suffering" or "curing ultimate biological disability."

The Left loves to deceive by using euphemisms, pretty words for ugly concepts, to make them more palatable to others. For instance, instead of "aborting an unborn baby" it becomes "removing the products of conception." Instead of "killing off useless people we don't want anymore" it becomes "helping those who can't help themselves." This is essentially a con game where the Left keeps much of the populace blissfully unaware of their own true intent, elicits their cooperation in things which sound good, and then it is too late when the majority wakes up and realizes the bitter consequences of the new law, program, or regulation. Euphemistically calling dog excrement "canine perfume" does not really make it smell any better.

In the case of euthanasia, no one—NO ONE—will be safe if the Left gets its way. There was another movement in the 1930's and

1940's, called National Socialism, which began by terminating the lives of people with horrible birth defects and severely retarded minds. That seemed oh so compassionate, oh so reasonable to many. But then the net of death spread more widely, to people of "inferior genetic stock," immoral behavior, gypsies, and then Jews. Germany's National Socialism in the time of Adolph Hitler is better known today as Nazism. They went all the way down the slippery slope very, very quickly.

Think it can't happen again? It's already happening in some "enlightened" countries abroad. The Netherlands is a few years further down the slippery euthanasia slope than America is. And already it has gotten so bad that older ill people in hospitals are sometimes "put out of their misery" like pitiful dogs, even when they expressly state they wish to live. Old people in the Netherlands are terrified to go to hospitals, for they know their docs may take the easier route of destroying them rather than trying to cure them.

That pattern will, absolutely without doubt, occur in America unless we actively counter the Left's propaganda and use the ballot box to prevent them implementing this agenda. In fact, it has already begun to happen here. There have been many cases, for instance, of docs deciding a newborn baby was too defective for a good future quality of life and leaving it uncared for to die...slowly and painfully without aid. We must cling ever to our constitutional rights and the Declaration of Independence with its ringing affirmation that our government exists only to protect our rights to "life, liberty, and the pursuit of happiness."

Therefore, a person should not have a legal right to actively destroy himself, for suicide is a form of homocide, but against one's own self. However, people should have the right to refuse "heroic" or extreme or experimental medical treatments, and let their terminal diseases run their natural course.

FEMINISM

THE LEFT: According to radical feminists, males have dominated virtually all societies forever and a day. They have oppressed women and created religions in their own image to provide justification for doing so. Thus the Judeo-Christian Bible portrays God in a male image and makes women subject to men. Christianity is hopelessly out of date and should be relegated to the dustbin of history. Society should get back to the female goddess side of religion, as was found in many pagan religions of long ago.

According to feminists, current society relegates women to more trivial or demeaning tasks and to lower status occupations and jobs. It discriminates against women who try to enter previously male careers and still enforces a "glass ceiling" which suppresses them from advancement to the upper levels of management in business, the military, etc. For every dollar the average male earns in the workplace, a woman earns only 73 cents. Sexual harassment is endemic in the workplace, and we should take great offense at even the most casual remark around the water cooler. If an older or more powerful male touches or has any sexual contact with a younger or less powerful female, it can be presumed as illegal sexual harassment, no matter how willing she may appear because she has no genuine freedom to say no. The only exception to this rule is a male politician like President Clinton who can do anything he wants as long as he politically supports abortion.

Marriage is a joke, just an institutionalized form of rape and further oppression for women. As one of the leading feminists of our age, Gloria Steinem, famously said, "A woman needs a man like a fish needs a bicycle." In terms of relationships, women can only feel safe when around other women. Many feminists see lesbianism as the only way to go, and many like Patricia Ireland, formerly president of NOW (National Organization for Women), have allegedly been lesbians, or at least bisexual.

Predatory, aggressive men are the bane of our culture and responsible for virtually every social problem, for example, wife battering, child abuse, abandonment of families, etc. Society would really just be better off if there were no men around.

In the Left's view, there really aren't any meaningful differences between the two genders at all, other than differences instilled culturally. A woman can do anything a man can do, and probably better in most cases. When little boys and little girls can be raised in a feminist-controlled environment, all differences will completely disappear, other than the obvious biological disparity in the sex organs.

Only the feminist movement, as exemplified by such organizations as NOW can be trusted to speak for women and to stand up for their rights. Consciousness raising sessions can help women—and enlightened men—realize the truth of all this.

THE RIGHT: There is no question that some societies have historically subjugated women, and some continue to do so. For example, in strict Muslim countries today, such as Saudi Arabia, and even more so in Afghanistan under the Taliban, females have essentially no rights at all, except as allowed by the males in their families. This is atrocious, ridiculous, and should be changed. But, oddly, today's feminists keep harping about American society, where they really have it pretty good, rather than other countries where the female half really is oppressed. Why are they so self-centered?

There is also no question that some individual men have taken advantage of this situation to exploit women for their own ends. But to see sin as something which only afflicts men and of which women are wholly innocent, is to be incredibly blind. Yes, some men batter their spouses or girlfriends. But what is almost completely overlooked is that some women batter their spouses or boyfriends. Yes, some fathers abuse their children, but so do some mothers. For every man in the workplace who actually harasses females, there is one or more females who either harass others or knowingly exploit harassment laws to intimidate men into giving them what they want. Using and abusing others for selfish reasons is not a distinctively male trait, it is a human trait which ALL humans need to resist.

And why do feminists turn into absolute shrieking harpies over alleged sexual harassment if it is in the military or by a conservative politician (e.g., the Navy's Tailhook incident, Supreme Court Justice Clarence Thomas, or Arnold Schwarzenegger) and remain strangely silent when it is by a liberal like President Clinton? There is a whopping double standard here, and it becomes clear they are not standing on general principles at all but are rather exploiting the issues of the day for their own political gain. This is just as much an abuse of power by the feminists as any of the abuse by men they so decry.

A religion that can be re-written by people of today to fit their own presuppositions has no more validity than a fairy tale. Either God has revealed Himself in Scriptures or He hasn't. It is either true or false. Seekers of God should try to determine the truth and adapt their views and beliefs accordingly, not try to re-write scripture to their own liking.

Interestingly, feminists in the past three decades or so have achieved just about every societal goal they began with, yet many find the victory a bitter and hollow one. For example, Gloria Steinem thought she would never want or need a man, yet got married in her old age. Countless women have sacrificed families for careers, only to regret it.

Feminists incessantly cite statistics about the so-called "gender gap" in wages but refuse to acknowledge the reason, which has nothing to do with sexism. In many career fields, e.g., the military, women and men in the same job with the same rank and years of experience, get exactly the same pay, down to the last penny. But women (or men for that matter) in private companies who choose easier jobs with flexible hours and no overtime, etc., will always make less than those who put career first and give their all to the company.

GAY AGENDA—See **HOMOSEXUALITY**

GOD—See **AMENDMENT, FIRST**

GOVERNMENT, Role Of

THE LEFT: Government is the savior of mankind. There is no earthly problem that enlightened, elite government leaders cannot solve. Too much poverty? We'll create Lyndon Johnson's War on Poverty and throw a couple of trillion dollars at the problem (a trillion is a thousand billion, or a million million). Education not doing too well? We'll create a Department of Education to solve all the problems. Too many racists in society? How about a Civil Rights Commission? Not enough private funding for the arts? How about a National Endowment of the Arts to make sure there is adequate funding for profane, anti-religious, and pro-homosexual "art" (such as the infamous crucifix in a jar of urine and Robert Mapplethorpe's homo-erotic photos)? Ditto for PBS (Public Broadcasting System) for TV and NPR (National Public Radio) for radio. Ditto for the National Endowment for the Humanities to make sure sociologists and others keep cranking out those textbooks calling for more and more government solutions. And of course, a big, powerful Internal Revenue Service to collect all the taxes needed to run such a behemoth, Hobbes' Leviathan.

The more centralized the government, the better. Power concentrated in the federal government is much more efficient and all-encompassing than that spread out among the states, the counties, the municipalities. To keep the latter in line, the Left will always attach strings to federal government largesse—the state, county, or city will only receive the money if they adhere to certain federal "standards," which usually is a code word for the politically correct, left-wing agenda.

The bigger the government, the better. The more functions the central government controls, the more likely it is that things will go the left-wing way. Leftists like big government, so big government jobs tend to attract leftists, which means that any major government bureaucracy (except the military) will likely have a majority of employees who tend left at least to some degree.

In the Left's view, the main obstacle is not the various societal problems themselves, but the people who are hopeless reactionaries, who cling to ridiculous outmoded beliefs and attitudes, "the vast right wing conspiracy" (to quote the Left's leading light, Hillary Clinton). Stupid conservatives are always trying to vote down government expansion and the raising of taxes. By some peculiar twist of fate, a huge percent of voters will listen to them rather than recognize the obviously superior wisdom of the leftist elite, so it is best not to confront them in free and open debate. Better to dema- gogue the issues and personally attack, and hopefully destroy, right wing opponents. The Left won't simply debate a conservative who wants to cut taxes, they will accuse him of being a racist, sexist, homophobic Nazi who wants to starve children and throw old people out into the street to die. Whereas ordinary voting citizens might listen to a conservative's logical argument to lower taxes, they will certainly recoil in horror from the monstrous Nazi bogey-man created in their imagination by leftist rhetoric. Then the Left will be free to keep expanding government, bigger and bigger, ad infini- tum...until complete socialism is achieved. See also **Socialism**.

THE RIGHT: America's Founding Fathers rightly recognized that big, centralized, all-powerful government is not the answer to America's problems, but rather a major cause of them. Thus they split up power into different branches of government, even at the federal level, so they could keep each other in line. They wrote a Constitution with a Bill of Rights which strictly limited what powers the Federal government would have (primarily over national defense), and which rights and powers would instead be held at the state level or in the hands of the citizenry themselves.

The Tenth Amendment in the Bill of Rights clearly states, "The powers not delegated to the United States by the Constitution, nor prohibited by it to the States, are reserved to the States respectively, or to the people." It has never been officially revoked or amended, yet it has been increasingly ignored over the last half century or so. Politicians now routinely assume power over some issue and federalize it, even when that power is clearly excluded to them by the U.S. Constitution. For example, the creation of so many federal agencies, as detailed on the previous page, required all three branches of government essentially to ignore the Constitution or to twist its meaning into saying something it really doesn't. For instance, nowhere in the Constitution is there a federal role over education, yet they have taken it over and made things...better? No! A heckuva lot worse!

Even sorrier than the issue of ignoring constitutional limitations is that the federal government has not bent the rules to make things better, but to make them worse! The large bureaucracies they create typically don't lessen the problem, but add to it! Johnson's War on Poverty spent trillions of tax dollars, but left us with not only an unsolved poverty problem, but the additional horrible problems attendant to a welfare state. For instance, when more poverty aid went to broken homes, it became in effect an incentive to have a broken home. So we had more and more broken homes, along with more people dropping out of school, turning to drugs and crime, because they lacked adequate parental figures while growing up. The poverty itself didn't worsen those problems; the government "solutions" did. Thankfully, conservatives in the 1990's began to reform welfare so as to encourage more responsible behavior rather than the left-wing approach of rewarding irresponsible behavior.

The Left constantly lives in a fantasy world where having noble intent is all that counts. They pat themselves on the back as having "compassion" because they are willing to throw other people's money at some societal problem, yet turn a blind eye when their policies make things incalculably worse for real people. That is not compassion. Conservatives try to live in the real world and consider the outcomes of their policies in real life. If a tough-love approach makes things actually better, they count that as more compassionate than the mere willingness to throw away someone else's money. Conservatives must not allow themselves to be silenced by overheated left-wing rhetoric and personal attacks. They must stick to the level of facts, not hyperbole like the Left; to the level of logic, not hysterical emotion; to real life, not flights of fantasy. Then real voters who respect actual solutions to problems will increasingly vote for them.

Government can never be the savior of mankind, and those who think it can will only make matters worse. The proper role of government is very limited to ensure personal freedom and domestic tranquility so that people can safely pursue their freely chosen goals and missions in life.

See also **CONSTITUTION, U.S.**

GUN CONTROL

THE LEFT: Letting ordinary people have access to guns gives them too much power. The common man is not to be trusted, so a wise, benevolent, but strong central government will certainly do everything it can to get rid of private ownership of guns. It is important to attack this problem from all directions simultaneously:

First, the Left's true intent—total disarmament of the public so there will be no defense against the coming one-world government—must be disguised in euphemisms which distract and reassure the citizenry. Instead, they'll pretend they want only "sensible" controls to reduce crime, always expressing the desire to protect children, etc. No one except for an idiot right-winger will openly oppose anything proposed in the name of helping "the children."

The Left must also prevent more guns from reaching the hands of the public. They'll use nuisance lawsuits against firearms manufacturing companies in an attempt to drive them out of business. They'll try to close down guns shows where guns are traded or purchased. They'll throw every bureaucratic impediment against an entrepreneur who wants to go into the gun business. They'll put more and more restrictions on the types of guns which can be produced and sold. They'll demand licensing, registration, and background checks.

At the same time the Left seeks to take away the guns that already exist, by such tactics as outlawing types of guns (e.g., the so-called "assault weapon" ban), implementing gun buyback programs, the development of registration lists, and pushing for outright confiscation. It is important to terrify the public about guns and gun owners so that ordinary folk will shun both and make the Left's job easier. Thus misleading and outright falsified statistics will be continually broadcast about the dangers of guns, and there will be a total ban in the mainstream media about reporting anything favorable about guns (e.g., how they are often used to stop crimes in progress).

There is still that pesky Second Amendment that gives people the right to gun ownership. That must be explained away by any means possible, including deliberate distortion of its plain meaning, claiming it only applies to the National Guard, and the spreading of absolute fabrications of history, such as Michael Bellesiles' ARMING AMERICA: THE ORIGINS OF A NATIONAL GUN CULTURE. Luckily for the Left the average person doesn't take the time to learn the facts and can easily be swayed by their propaganda.

There will always be conservatives who will tell the truth and oppose the Left's agenda, and they must be relentlessly attacked and mischaracterized as "gun nuts" who want machine pistols in every child's lunchbox and who would re-create a dangerous "wild west" with its shootouts and duels in the streets.

THE RIGHT: The Founding Fathers enshrined in the Constitution a right they considered second in importance only to the freedom of speech and religion, the right to guns. Here are their exact words in the Second Amendment to the Bill of Rights:

"A well regulated Militia, being necessary to the security of a free State, the right of the people to keep and bear Arms shall not be infringed."

The Left constantly tries to misinterpret this amendment despite the fact that scores of Supreme Court decisions over the past couple of hundred years have repeatedly stressed it means that gun owner-ship is an individual right (e.g., see the book, SUPREME COURT GUN CASES: TWO CENTURIES OF GUN RIGHTS REVEALED). The Left claims that the preamble referring to the Militia means it applies, in today's terms, to the National Guard. That is not only incorrect, it is just plain ignorant. No colonial American could possibly imagine needing a Constitutional amendment to spec-ify that the Militia could have weapons--what else would they fight with? Bare fists? The key phrase is not "a well regulated Militia" but "the right of the people." The right to arms is given to "the people," the same "people" to which all the other rights of the first ten amend-ments are given. All of them are individual rights.

So why did the Founding Fathers consider this right so essen-tial? So people could hunt or go target shooting? No, but rather so there would be a vast majority of the people skilled in firearms use and in their possession so that they could, if necessary, resist invasion or the imposition of tyranny either from without or within the country. The whole able-bodied and willing populace should thus have the means to preserve their freedom—that is the meaning of the term "militia," not a separate, small, uniformed, and professional armed force.

Is it possible, then, to consider this amendment outmoded in an age where guns are used so often in crime? Quite the opposite. The Left touts only stats showing the danger of guns, such as how many youth are annually killed with guns. (They always call them "children," creating an image of innocent kids finding a parental gun in the home and accidentally shooting someone, but the vast majority are actually teenage gang members deliberately engaging in mayhem). But they (and the elite mainstream media) totally ignore the approximately 2.5 *million* times a year that guns are used annually in the U.S. to prevent or stop a crime in progress (as reported by Florida State University criminologist Dr. Gary Kleck). Most of the time, the victim need only brandish a gun to send the criminal fleeing. In Switzerland, nearly every home has one of the Left's dreaded "assault weapons," a concept quite in keeping with "the militia" as explained above, and the result has been a long unbroken period of peace and freedom and a very low crime rate. States in the U.S. which introduce expanded "right to carry" (gun) laws see a decrease in crime as a result. Countries such as Great Britain and Australia which follow the Left's prescription of gun registration followed by confiscation immediately see a dramatic and horrid escalation in the gun crime rate. Washington, DC has some of the toughest anti-gun laws in the nation, but their murder rate is 45 times as high as South Dakota where the majority of homes have guns. As is often said, "when guns become criminal, only criminals have guns," and they feel freer to use them knowing their victims are unarmed. Yet America's current 20,000 gun laws (counting federal, state, and local) are not considered enough and the Left wants more...always more. Hitler, Stalin, and other recent dictators have also been big fans of gun control, because they knew that disarming the populace was an essential first step to enslaving them.

HOMOSEXUALITY

THE LEFT: To liberals, everything "Gay is okay!" No one has a right to impose their morality or homophobic religious beliefs on anyone else. Sex is a natural part of life and any way you want to express it is just fine. In fact, it is more healthy to express your sexuality, however different or atypical it is, than to inhibit yourself. Expression is good; inhibition is downright unhealthy and dangerous. It leads to all sorts of mental and emotional problems. That's why the Left must do everything possible to destroy middle class sexual mores—they stand in the way of human fulfillment and personal growth.

So it is okay to insist that right-wing, inhibited homophobes cannot impose their morality on everyone else; but it is also okay for the Left to impose their amoral viewpoint on the rest of society. This is an area where double standards are not only permissible but absolutely necessary. The Left knows best and must make its viewpoint the only one allowed to be heard in public. The Left must squelch the Right in every way possible to make sure they can not spread their homophobia any farther.

Thus we must criminalize not only overt actions of violence against gays, but also speech, attitudes, and even religious beliefs that there is anything wrong with homosexuality. A little wordplay can help here, as the Left finesses constitutional issues of free speech and again employs euphemisms to disarm the enemy and confuse the muddled majority in the middle. Thus any display of disagreement with the gay agenda becomes a "hate crime." Any verbalized expression which is less than eager endorsement of the gay lifestyle becomes "gay bashing" and "homophobia." That is really clever wordplay there, because the former implies that even the mildest attitudes against something are really a form of violence, or at least as bad as actual violence. The latter is a diabolical stroke of genius, because it makes it sound as if the right wing is not merely wrong but actually mentally ill, crazy, hopelessly out of it. No evidence of that is required, of course, just the constant audacious chanting of it.

This strategy of personal attacks works because it makes most who disagree with the Left afraid to speak out, and gives the impression to those who are unsure what to believe that only the Left's view is worth listening to. In so doing they can create an environment in which it is okay for everyone else to hate the "haters" while at the same time priding themselves on their marvelous "tolerance."

There is still the pesky problem of AIDS, which began largely as a gay disease and, even though it has spread among other subgroups such as drug users, prostitutes, promiscuous heterosexuals, other sexual partners of those with HIV/AIDS, and occasionally the recipients of tainted blood transfusions, it is still largely identified with the gay population. The best tactic here, again, is to displace the blame—don't let anyone ever imply that it is gay behavior as such that spreads the disease, but rather blame the right wing, the people who oppose acceptance of homosexuality. For instance, the Left can keep blaming it on ex-President Ronald Reagan or Jerry Falwell, even though they did nothing to actually cause AIDS, and if radicals scream the Big Lie often enough and vehemently enough, people will start to believe it.

THE RIGHT: God created humankind and made them male and female. He made their bodies, minds, and souls and knows what is best for their health and happiness. To make sure humans knew what was best for them, He wrote them a beautiful instruction book. No one makes people follow the rules, but they will be healthier and happier when they do. Breaking the rules against homosexuality makes as much sense as sticking pancakes and syrup into your VCR. You may think it is cool or neat, you may enjoy the thrill of breaking the rules, but you still pay the penalty of screwing up your system. The Left turns a blind eye to that basic fact and wants to compel society to extol the virtues of pancakes and syrup in VCRs and to rewrite all the manuals to teach that is a noble use of VCRs and to punish and marginalize anyone who dares timidly to disagree. But no amount of political shenanigans, votes in legislative bodies, or left-wing judicial decisions for "gay marriage", etc., etc., can change the fact than unnatural behavior has consequences. You may as well vote to stop the moon from appearing at night or to ban cancer by fiat. The gay lifestyle, particularly among males, leads not only to such possibilities as HIV/AIDS, but also other sexually transmitted diseases (STDs), hepatitis, gay bowel syndrome, and an endless list of others. On average, a promiscuous male gay lifestyle cuts the normal lifespan about in half.

The Right does not, for the most part, hate gays at all. There are some gay bashers who actually do engage in violence against gays, but they are criminals just like any others and are not emblematic of the peaceful people on the right. The vast majority of conservatives have compassion for gays and wish them well, not by endorsing their chosen path to self-destruction, but by pointing out its dangers. Conservatives are standing before a washed-out bridge with signs saying "BRIDGE OUT AHEAD" while homosexuals race towards their own doom. To compassionately try to help gays is not homophobia, which means an irrational, neurotic fear of homosexuals. If anything, it would be more accurate to call the Left "religiophobes" or "Christophobes," because they really are terrified of Christianity and how its no-nonsense proclamation of the truth pricks their consciences.

The Left sometimes claims that gays wouldn't have any problems at all if only society would accept them as being fully normal and wonderful in every way, just as they are, and in no need of changing anything about themselves. If mere philosophical disagreement can cause such problems, what about the Left's continual vehement and strident opposition against conservatives? Their unbridled hostility and arrogant sense of superiority does not affect us one whit; so why should our polite and subdued mere disagreement bother them so? Could it be they know we are right but are terrified that anything remind them of that? They are so desperately trying to fool themselves that any hint they are wrong becomes unbearable. If they truly believed they were right, way deep down in every fiber of their beings, then the disagreement of others would be trivial and insignificant. But, of course, they don't truly believe it, for the God who created them instilled in them a basic awareness of the ultimate truth of right and wrong. They can deny it, can run and hide from it, can viciously attack those who remind them of it, but can't erase it.

The latest push in the gay agenda is for homosexual marriage, but before we rush down the road to Sodom and Gomorrah, look what acceptance of gay unions has done to Scandinavia, which is about 15 or so years ahead of us on this issue. It did not lead to gay commitment and monogamy, as is so often claimed, but has effectively destroyed heterosexual marriage. Couples of all possible gender combinations tend to disrespect and shun marriage and just live together instead. The occasional conservative couple who believes in marriage is embarrassed to admit it.

HUMANISM

THE LEFT: Radical humanists believe that now that all thinking folk have realized that God is "dead," i.e., he never existed and man finally comprehends it, we can put Man up on the pedestal where he belongs. Man becomes, in effect, his own god. There is nothing higher, though humankind continues to evolve and will become ever more god-like.

So we can dispense with all religions and all silly religious "do's" and "don'ts." Humans can freely create their own values and purposes with no outside interference. Some of the tenets of this areligious religion, as expressed in the Humanist Manifesto II (1973), include that religion is bogus, man arose by evolution, consenting adults should be free to practice sex any way they want, and we need a one-world government to replace individual nations. Humanist Manifesto 2000 stresses even more the importance of one, united, global world, with its apt subtitle "A Call for a New Planetary Humanism," and frequent references to globalism throughout.

The following is a quote from "A Secular Humanist Declaration" issued in 1980 by the Council for Democratic and Secular Humanism (now the Council for Secular Humanism, which can be found at website www.secularhumanism.org):

"As secular humanists, we are generally skeptical about supernatural claims... We are doubtful of traditional views of God and divinity... we find that traditional views of the existence of God either are meaningless, have not yet been demonstrated to be true, or are tyrannically exploitative. Secular humanists may be agnostics, atheists, rationalists, or skeptics, but they find insufficient evidence for the claim that some divine purpose exists for the universe. They reject the idea that God has intervened miraculously in history or revealed himself to a chosen few or that he can save or redeem sinners. They believe that men and women are free and are responsible for their own destinies and that they cannot look toward some transcendent Being for salvation. We reject the divinity of Jesus, the divine mission of Moses, Mohammed, and other latter day prophets and saints of the various sects and denominations. We do not accept as true the literal interpretation of the Old and New Testaments, the Koran, or other allegedly sacred religious documents, however important they may be as literature. Religions are pervasive sociological phenomena, and religious myths have long persisted in human history....We have found no convincing evidence that there is a separable "soul" or that it exists before birth or survives death. We must therefore conclude that the ethical life can be lived without the illusions of immortality or reincarnation. Human beings can develop the self confidence necessary to ameliorate the human condition and to lead meaningful, productive lives."

THE RIGHT: Humanists claim to be skeptics about religion in the sense of belief in god, but they actually are firm believers in their own religion of secular humanism, with religion here referring to a system of beliefs one holds to explain reality. Humanists claim to believe in the separation of church and state, but what they really want is to have their belief system, their "religion" enshrined as the legal law of the land. Only their religion will be allowed a public hearing and will thus be "established" as the official state viewpoint, a clear violation of the First Amendment.

No belief in the supernatural allowed. No study of creationism or mention of God in school permitted. No discussion of biblical morality accepted. This is tolerance? Conservatives don't think so. The Humanist Elite are very much like the authoritarian High Priests and mullahs of various other religions. It is "their way or the highway." Don't you dare try to sneak in any religious or moral viewpoints on such issues as abortion, homosexuality, or euthanasia. They assume in advance that you have no validity, just like the rigid religious elite of times past who would brook no challenge to their orthodoxy.

Look, for instance, at the snide references to religion in the quote above. "They find insufficient evidence" for the reality of god and thus dismiss the topic outright. What about the millions upon millions of people who do see such evidence all around them? Any such person is deemed to be a victim of "pervasive sociological phenomena and religious myths," in other words, an idiot or bigot at best who is not yet "enlightened" as they themselves, the liberal elite, are.

How about this for a myth with a total lack of directly observable evidence? A bunch of inert chemicals were just sitting around eons ago and got charged with energy by a bolt of lightning and somehow became a living precursor to a cell! All by themselves! And then, instead of almost immediately reverting back to a non-living condition, they grew and multiplied and specialized, and evolved with billions and billions of *accidental* changes into the unbelievably complex and interconnected web of hundreds of thousands of species we know today, with the pinnacle of that evolution being an incredibly advanced and complex species whose members…generally believe in God. What an incredible bunch of accidents!

So…an amazingly complex and intricate creation doesn't imply a creator, an agent of Intelligent Design? No, of course not! Next time you see a beautiful sculpture, don't bother to look for a creator's name, just assume that wind and water erosion over the eons just naturally shaped it. And it doesn't really have any more beauty and meaning than any other random pile of rocks. Random creation by evolution is one of the foundational tenets of the fundamentalist believers at the Orthodox Church of Secular Humanism. And don't you dare challenge them unless you want the Humanist Inquisition to (metaphorically) burn your career at the stake!

For further discussion of select aspects of the Humanists' fully Established Religion of Secularism, see **SEXUALITY** and **UN**.

INCOME REDISTRIBUTION—See **TAXATION**

ISRAEL

THE LEFT: When the Nazi Party (AKA the National Socialist Party of Germany) was butchering Jews by the millions, it was possible for enlightened liberals to feel some sympathy for them. When World War II ended, the UN Special Committee on Palestine (UNSCOP) recommended the re-creation of a modern nation of Israel, in the region of the original nation of Israel, right smack in the middle of Palestine. The UN General Assembly in 1947 voted to partition Palestine into a Jewish and a separate Arab state, but when Arabs in the region began to revolt against the plan, Israel declared its own independence in 1948 and was immediately recognized by most UN members such as the U.S.

In its brief history, modern Israel has had to fight several wars even to survive, e.g., in 1948, 1967, and 1973. And in recent years they have struggled to suppress an Intifida, an uprising of radical Palestinians, including suicide bombers, in and around their borders. And herein lies the problem. Enlightened leftists no longer have much sympathy for Israel, for they have taken over Arab territory and are suppressing minorities who also yearn to breathe free. Israel should instead carve out of their territory an independent Palestinian state for these displaced Arabs and should abide by the various international accords meant to ensure peace in the Middle East.

That they have not done so proves, in the Left's view, that Israel is the greatest threat to peace in the world. No wonder anti-Semitism is actually on the rise again among leftist intellectuals and others throughout Europe and even the U.S. The United Nations regularly condemns Israel as such, and it is way past time for the United States to stop supporting Israel militarily and politically and to push them towards accepting the inevitable.

For instance, an Associated Press report on April 16, 2003 began with, "The United Nations Human Rights Commission yesterday overwhelmingly condemned Israel for "mass killing" of Palestinians, and for its settlement policy in the territories. The

United States was alone in voting against all four resolutions, saying that the criticism of Israel was one-sided and unfair. The resolutions followed impassioned arguments earlier in the commission's annual session during which Palestinian delegate Nabil Ramlawi claimed that Israel used forms of killings and torture which "were worse than the practices of Nazism." The comments caused an outcry among Jewish groups. Israel is regularly condemned by the 53-nation commission - the top UN human rights body - which this year is chaired by Libyan Ambassador Najat Al-Hajjaji."

THE RIGHT: Never before in history has the people of an ancient nation been scattered all over the world (the Diaspora) and then gathered back to their original homeland thousands of years later to recreate a modern form of their long past nation...just as the Bible foretold centuries ago. When the Jews first began to return in large numbers in the early decades of last century, what was to become Israel was largely useless desert, more suitable for nomadic Bedouins than modern civilization. But the Jews rolled up their sleeves and went to work reclaiming the desert and making the cracked, dry soil bloom again. They built modern cities and welcomed refugees from both the free and oppressed nations of the world.

There is something very special about Israel. Even those who reject the proposition that the Jews are God's Chosen People usually can't fail to notice the people's spirit, their motivation, industry, and sense of purpose. Israel is an oasis of democracy surrounded by Arab/Muslim dictatorships or monarchies (some, like Jordan, are currently quite benign, while others like Syria sponsor terrorism against Israel). While many American Christians are staunch supporters of Israel on biblical grounds, even those without a religious view of the issue should recognize that the United States should always remain a close friend and loyal supporter of Israel as the only democracy and the best supporter of the West in the region.

When the openly stated aim of many of Israel's local enemies is to "drive them into the Sea," i.e., kill the Jews and destroy Israel as a Jewish homeland, it is understandable that Israel maintains a strong military and is quick to employ it against terrorists. Israel can't sit idly by, blindly accepting peace proposals and treaties when there is a chance these are just shams meant to lull them into a false sense of security so their enemies can more easily vanquish them. In the 1967 war, for example, Israel's population was out-numbered by Arabs about 50 to one, while the Soviet Union had generally trained and armed its adversaries (the U.S. had militarily prepared Israel). Hesitation or indecision in the face of odds like that could have spelled doom. And still could.

When various Muslim terrorist groups are continually attacking Israel with suicide bombers and other despicable means, how can anyone believe they sincerely want a peace which includes the continuing survival of Israel? Which side is morally superior is clearly seen in that one deliberately blows up pizza parlors and hotels and buses filled with civilians and innocent men, women, and children, while the other (Israel) uses measured military force only against specific targets of armed terrorists and other hostiles.

The U.S. must never forget who the "good guys" are in this conflict and must always support Israel.

JUDICIARY

THE LEFT: An activist judiciary is the Left's last hope to implement its agenda. In recent decades, it has been extraordinarily difficult for an openly left candidate to win the presidency. Witness, for example, the stunning defeat of McGovern in 1972 and of Mondale in 1984. Democratic candidates who have won the presidency in recent decades have campaigned as moderates. Clinton, for example, pretended to be a centrist and did, in fact, go along with the GOP on a number of issues such as welfare reform, though at heart he seemed to be more a leftist than he let on. At any rate, the hardcore Left has generally had a hard time keeping a firm grasp on the executive branch.

Ditto for the legislative branch. Left-leaning states such as New York do elect hard-left candidates like Hillary Clinton. But in most states, particularly the South and Midwest, leftists have to pretend to be something else to win. When the sheep's clothing is removed and the true wolf within revealed, it is fairly easy for the electorate to rid themselves of a left-wing senator or representative in Congress.

Not so for the judicial branch. The Left can readily count on its presidents to nominate only left-wing judges for the higher federal courts and for its senators to stop at nothing either to get leftist judicial activists voted in, or at least to prevent strict constructionist candidates, those who interpret the Constitution as it is actually written, from being voted in. Once a Supreme Court justice has been sworn in, he can vote hard left for the rest of his career and implement huge portions of the left-wing agenda against the will of the majority, with the angry and disillusioned populace having no hope of voting him out. Federal judges can remain in office for life, unless impeached for specific crimes.

Even judges nominated by conservative presidents can often be turned gradually towards the left. Most every professional in every field likes to be appreciated by his peers and approved by the media and other elite trendsetters. A conservative Supreme Court justice who, for example, begins to support abortion issues will get flattering reviews from the New York Times and other news outlets, reinforcement which begins to turn them ever more leftward. On the other hand, it takes incredible courage and commitment to remain true to one's original principles in the face of non-stop criticism and character assassination by the media elite as, for example, Justice Clarence Thomas has always endured. And the cultural elite will never applaud a leftist judge for moving towards the right, so that will never happen.

So the Judiciary is the Left's "Custer's Last Stand." They will stop at nothing to block a nominee who believes in the actual U.S. Constitution. A vicious campaign which makes mountains out of molehills, parades questionable witnesses of alleged wrongdoing, or slanders with unfounded rumors has come to be known as "borking," so-named for Supreme Court nominee Judge Robert Bork, who was successfully blocked in 1987, simply because he believed in the actual Constitution written by the Founding Fathers. More recently, when Senate Judiciary Committee liberals realize they don't have enough votes to kill a nomination, they simply use filibuster threats to keep the candidate from getting an open up-or-down vote in the full Senate.

THE RIGHT: It is appalling and fundamentally dishonest how the Left continues to short circuit the democratic process by evading the clear will of the majority of the people by turning to extremist, activist federal judges to implement their agenda.

The Founding Fathers never intended for the judiciary to become that powerful. It is supposed to interpret the laws, not make them, not legislate from the bench. Thomas Jefferson warned repeatedly that we had not enough protection against judicial tyranny: "Over the Judiciary department, the Constitution [has] deprived [the people] of their control. ... The original error [was in] establishing a judiciary independent of the nation, and which, from the citadel of the law, can turn its guns on those they were meant to defend, and control and fashion their proceedings to its own will...." Jefferson's prophecy, unfortunately, was right on target.

Many left-wing judges have become tyrants, despots, imposing their own extremist views on the rest of society with just a passing pretense at actually finding what they want in the printed words of the Constitution. For instance, all over the country, the ACLU and like-minded groups are rushing to court to have public monuments of the Ten Commandments removed, and often judges rule in their favor under the pretext of separation of church and state. This is blatantly absurd in that merely posting the Ten Commandments does not establish an official religion, it simply recognizes the historical importance of those ten in the historical development of our own laws, and, moreover, the U.S. Supreme Court building itself has those emblazoned in stone. Are leftists really trying to pretend that U.S. laws against stealing and murder have no historical foundation but just sprang out of George Washington's head as brand new thoughts?

Or take the issue of leftists trying to remove the phrase "under God" from the Pledge of Allegiance. Even though no one is forced to say those two words if they are offended by them, the Ninth Circuit Court of Appeals ruled that it was unconstitutional for anyone to say those words and they should therefore be struck from the Pledge. The U.S. Senate voted 99 to 0 and the House of Representatives voted 416 to 3 in support of the Pledge as it is, but such resolutions are not binding on the court—they are merely suggestions.

The Senate is allowed by the U.S. Constitution only the role of "advise and consent" in the federal judge appointment process. That means they should ensure that nominees are properly qualified and then approve them. That does not give them the right to apply political correctness as a litmus test to ensure they will defy the people and consistently vote hard left, legislating from the bench. That does not give them the right to consistently exclude the very people who would honestly do their jobs of applying the real Constitution, for fear that the Left won't win in an honest debate.

Conservatives think it is way, way past time for the other two branches of government to begin restoring the balance of powers and restricting the judiciary to its proper constitutional role. And it is way, way past time for the public to use the ballot box, as well as email, letter, and phone campaigns to force their senators to give a fair hearing to judicial nominees who are willing to do their sworn duty of upholding the actual Constitution, rather than pretending it says whatever they want.

See also **CONSTITUTION, U.S.**

MARRIAGE—See **SEXUALITY**

MEDIA BIAS

THE LEFT: The media aren't biased towards liberalism or the left at all. Right-wingers are always criticizing the media for left-wing bias, but it simply isn't accurate, according to media liberals. Responsible reporters and newscasters simply call the facts as they see them. Such professionals can lay aside their own feelings about an issue, if they have any, and objectively report the facts.

If anything, the Left claims there is a right-wing bias in the media. No matter how much dirt the Left could dredge up on President Reagan, for example, the media kept portraying him as a friendly, likeable old man. No matter how the Left has raged against President Bush in the early years of his tenure, he hasn't yet been hounded from office. Newspapers like the Washington Times and the Wall Street Journal consistently skew to the right. As the incredibly brilliant and talented First Lady Hillary Clinton bravely stated, there is indeed a "vast right wing conspiracy" funded by billionaires such as Richard Mellon Scaife. Magazines such as The American Spectator made a name for themselves by reporting in depth on all the Clinton "scandals." Businessmen like Rupert Murdoch own way too many media outlets that generally toe the conservative line.

Fox TV News panders to the Right and has thus shot up in their ratings. Liberals feel it is shameful how they have stolen the audience from responsible telenews stations like CNN. In general, when conservatives comment on the news they are clearly displaying right-wing bias and their own prejudices. Liberals know in advance they can count on them to be racists, sexists, homophobic, militaristic, and jingoistic.

Bernard Goldberg, formerly of the mainstream media himself, is a traitor in the Left's eyes for writing best-selling exposes on media leftwing bias such as the books BIAS and ARROGANCE: RESCUING AMERICA FROM THE MEDIA ELITE. He has no business providing inside information as ammunition for the Right.

THE RIGHT: Left-wing media bias was so complete, so universal, so omnipresent for so many decades that left-wingers apparently didn't even notice it. To them, having only the left-wing view and nothing else but the left-wing view in public discourse was so ordinary that it didn't stand out but faded into the background like a blue sky or the air we breathe or speaking in English on American TV. It was just natural, just part of the normal cultural milieu, just the way things were.

This naturally left conservatives feeling alone, isolated, shut out of the mainstream of normal society. Each conservative or small cluster of conservatives tended to feel like the famed "Elephant Man" of 19th century London. They felt odd, weird, like freaks who would never be accepted in public at all if seen openly for what they really were. Essentially all conservatives tended to keep their opinions to themselves or within a small circle of friends they could trust. Particularly when going to college or applying for professional jobs, they generally learned to keep their true beliefs unspoken. Day after day, when exposed to the media or pronouncements from the cultural elite, they learned to suffer in silent amazement as everyone else but them seemed to be saying and believing stupid or false things which contravened all common sense and their own personal experience, yet were never contradicted openly. Everyone else seemed to believe the Emperor of liberalism had on beautiful, wondrous garments, while only the solitary conservative himself seemed aware that the Emperor was not only naked, but quite ugly and grotesque as well.

For decades, all one ever heard on the media were left-wing views such as: guns are always bad and dangerous, they directly cause crimes such as mass murders and should be banned; prayer or other signs of belief in God must be eliminated from every public venue; whatever the most strident feminists claim must be true; reverse racism (affirmative action) is a good thing; people must be free to have sex with whomever they want, however they want, and with unlimited partners; capitalists (businessmen) are greedy, selfish and evil, while socialists and communists are idealists and reformers who love "the people"; the traditional family is not only useless and irrelevant but downright harmful, such that any combination of people who want to live together should be considered a family; kids don't need their biological parents but will do better with an amorphous "village" of daycare and government bureaucrats; homelessness becomes an intolerable problem if a conservative is president but is somehow unnoticed if a liberal sits in the Oval Office; more government is the answer to all problems, and we should be happy our taxes are going up because that means we'll get more government solutions and life will just keep getting better; the military is shameful and rotten and not to be trusted, but rather we should rely on pacifism and unilateral disarmament; every other culture on earth has better qualities than America and Israel and we should learn from them, a religious or conservative person in a TV show or movie is always a hypocrite and one of the bad guys, etc., ad nauseum.

It was not until the advent of Rush Limbaugh and other conservative talk show hosts, and later the internet, that conservatives began to realize they weren't alone. The liberal cultural monolith began to crumble. Only in recent years have savvy businessmen realized there actually is a market out there for something other than universal liberal blather and are starting to fill that niche, though still with only a few magazines, newspapers, TV and radio stations. Even now the generic mainstream media dominates the nation and continues to be unabashedly leftist...without apparently even realizing it.

MILITARY

THE LEFT: The military is not to be trusted, rather it is to be loathed and despised. People either in uniform or who support the military are imperialistic warmongers who want to oppress the peoples of the Third World and steal their assets such as oil.

All the political speeches about liberating Iraq or restoring democracy in Haiti or Panama or Grenada are just double talk, in the Left's view. The U.S. doesn't intervene militarily in situations such as Rwanda, during the Tutsi vs Hutu tribe genocide there, where America had nothing to gain. But they send the troops into places such as Kuwait and Iraq where there are millions of barrels of oil just waiting to be taken. Reagan was an imperialistic nut case for escalating the arms race with the former Soviet Union.

The Left's road to peace is not from militarism but rather unilateral disarmament. If we would instead just lay down our arms, demobilize the troops, and eliminate the military-industrial complex, we would prove to the world that we want peace and are no threat to them. Then they would love us and the world could live in harmony at last.

Liberals love to imagine what America could do with the money wasted on armaments. Why, just the billions spent on a single weapons system such as aircraft carriers or stealth bombers could revitalize day care across the nation or provide free abortions to all the needy women who want them. Congress is always having debates about spending the budget on "guns vs. butter," i.e., weapons vs. socially good things. Debate over. The military budget should be drastically slashed, if not eliminated altogether, and everything should be put into social welfare. We don't need individual nations with their bickering militaries, anyway. As the visionary John Lennon of the Beatles sang:

> "Imagine there's no countries
> It isn't hard to do
> Nothing to kill or die for
> And no religion too

Imagine all the people
Living life in peace...
You may say I'm a dreamer
But I'm not the only one
I hope someday you'll join us
And the world will be as one."

The way to go is elimination of individual countries with their jingoistic calls to patriotism and preparations for war. With a single, one-world government we will finally achieve global peace. Till then, the United Nations is our best hope for international cooperation, and if we allow any military activity at all, it must go only through them with multilateral approval. No exceptions.

THE RIGHT: The only tangible thing on earth standing between America's unique experiment in constitutional freedom and invasion followed by tyranny and enslavement is America's first class, unparalleled military.

In the late 1970's, President Carter gutted our military and chose the path of appeasement and showing weakness as a way to win peace, but instead democracy declined all over the world as tyrants marched into the vacuum. The Soviet Union invaded Afghanistan, the Cubans took over Grenada and fomented strife throughout much of Africa, and the pro-western Shah of Iran was overthrown by a radical Islamic theocracy. And did they love us for stepping aside and letting them take over? NO! Iranian militants denounced America as "the Great Satan," and did something unprecedented—took over the U.S. Embassy in Tehran and kept our diplomats and embassy staff as hostages for 444 days.

President Reagan, by contrast, believed in peace through strength. Iran, knowing Reagan would not sit idly by once he became Commander-in-Chief, released our hostages on the very day of Reagan's inauguration. Reagan rebuilt our military and won the Cold War as a direct result, his predictions of the dissolution of the Soviet Union coming true shortly after he left office. Around the world, communism and other tyranny receded and freedom advanced as Reagan and then the elder Bush aided Afghanistan and freed Grenada and Panama and Kuwait, and assisted democratic efforts around the globe.

In the new war on terrorism, Clinton showed weakness in Somalia and also after terror attacks at U.S. installations in the Mideast and on the USS Cole and at our embassies in Africa. This emboldened the likes of Osama bin Laden and led to an escalation of terror, culminating in the horrendous 9/11 attacks of 2001. But President Bush the younger showed resolve and flexed our military might, and overthrew sadistic tyrannies in Afghanistan and Iraq. Did showing military backbone make Islamic fanatics hate us any more? They already had the maximum hate possible, but they learned a new respect for America. Suddenly Libya, Iran, Sudan, North Korea, and elsewhere became a lot more concerned about being cooperative with Uncle Sam.

Having a strong military is not the same as being militaristic. America is decidedly not imperialistic in the sense of wanting to conquer other countries and take over their territory and steal their assets, a la Germany and Japan in World War II. There is all the difference in the world between using military action to conquer and to liberate, and leftists who can't see that are deliberately being blind. The best means "to secure peace is to prepare for war," as Karl von Clausewitz once said. Individual members of the military tend to be model citizens, patriotic, responsible, and generous. They of all people are not eager for war and killing, for they will bear the brunt of the burden in any military action. But they realize that the security of the nation and their children's hopes for future freedom lie not in appeasing bullies and tyrants, but in opposing them. All the budgetary "butter" issues, all the day care centers in the world, won't be of much help if terrorists are allowed to freely rain down death and destruction on America. True, America doesn't intervene in every conflict in the world, it can't spread itself too thin, but there is nothing wrong with giving priority to situations which directly affect us.

PATRIOTISM—See **AMERICA**

POLITICAL CORRECTNESS

THE LEFT: Back in the 1950's, the Ike years, TV's "HAPPY DAYS" period, people were generally conservative but also uptight, inhibited, and close-minded. What with McCarthyism and other anti-communism, it was almost impossible for a leftist to get an open hearing in public. Even in the 60's radicals had to demonstrate on campus, staging sit-ins in administrative buildings, and marching in the city streets to get attention.

On college campuses, the Left basically appealed to fairness—it wasn't fair for the right-wing reactionary faculty and administrators to try to squelch protests or prevent young people from expressing their beliefs. In the immortal words of the 1966 revolutionary song, FOR WHAT IT'S WORTH (by Stephen Stills), "Young people speaking their minds, Are getting so much resistance from behind." Free speech had to be granted to lefties also.

The strategy worked, particularly as the Viet Nam era war and draft fueled ever larger and more vehement protests in the late 60's and early 70's. The campus hierarchies began to crumble before the opposition and give in to one student demand after another. Even the briefest of glances at high school and college yearbooks throughout the period showed the rapid change. Earlier student photos showed clean-cut, short-haired men, with both sexes in conservative clothes. Later photos showed long-haired hippies, beards, and outlandishly psychedelic clothing and adornments.

When that 60's generation of radical students grew up to become the hard-left professors and campus administrators in the 80's and beyond, they decided to consolidate their power. Now that they had total control of most campuses, they wanted to keep it that way. Out the window went free speech and the right to dissent. Gone was the notion of fairness in letting the opposition express itself. The Left wanted no tactics available by which the tiny conservative minority on campus could launch a counter-revolution.

So they began, like rigid ecclesiastical authorities in ages past, to dictate what the orthodox, allowable views on certain issues could be, and to not merely not tolerate dissent but actively squelch it by outlawing certain words and actions as "hate speech," and condemning and even punishing anyone who dared to disagree. Therefore, it became politically correct only to heartily endorse all aspects of the homosexual agenda (anything less became illegal and immoral gay-bashing and "homophobia"); to assert that every form of reverse discrimination was only proper and just (else you'd be branded a racist); to agree with every whim of the radical feminists no matter how extreme and nonsensical (else you'd be creamed as a sexist). Etc., etc.

"Tolerance" became a code word for "full and 100% agreement with all aspects of the Left's agenda," else the High Priests of "tolerance" would become absolutely and totally intolerant of you mighty fast. No dissension allowed.

THE RIGHT: It is amazing how leftists who claim to believe in free speech really mean it only if it applies to them. No one who disagrees with the Left's orthodoxy is given the same courtesy in return. At best, this is extremely childish, a kind of "heads I win; tails you lose" approach. At worst, it can be sordidly destructive and un-American, a clear violation of everything the U.S. Constitution stands for.

Many university campuses across the land have become, in political terms at least, little tinpot Marxist dictatorships where the Bill of Rights has no local jurisdiction. Political atrocities such as the following are unfortunately common:

- A campus newspaper boldly publishes an article by a conservative criticizing some aspect of the Politically Correct (PC) orthodoxy, and lefties seize the entire printing of the paper and destroy it. They further have the nerve to call this an exercise in free speech, meaning their own right to free speech, of course. But as this episode illustrates, the Left generally knows it can't win in open, honest debate so instead short circuits that by silencing their opposition by any means possible. Further, as this event unfolded at the University of Pennsylvania, President Sheldon Hackney not only failed to discipline the lefties for their egregious violations against the conservatives, he instead disciplined the security guard who attempted to stop the leftists from destroying private property.

- Conservative students put placards up on campus to announce their group meetings or a speech by an invited well-known conservative speaker. The placards are torn down by liberals, again claiming their own right to free speech in doing so.

- Conservative speakers like Supreme Court Justice Clarence Thomas are invited to speak, but when the local liberal harpies get wind of it, they shriek and threaten until the invitation is withdrawn.

- A student dares to criticize the PC dogma on affirmative action and is not merely branded a racist but is brought up on charges by the campus "Thought Police" for violations of the campus Speech Code.

- Every left-wing group imaginable on campus gets student funding, but not any Christian or politically conservative group, which may actually be banned from organizing on campus at all.

The examples could go on and on. Political correctness has gone amuck not only on campuses from coast to coast, but in newsrooms, government bureaus, and generally almost anywhere that the cultural elite gather or maintain control. It is way past time for the majority with common sense to stand up to these bullies and insist that the Bill of Rights applies to all...not just the leftist PC elite.

POLITICS

THE LEFT: The hard Left wants political power and is willing to pay almost any price to get it. They realize they are a minority in the country and that they can't honestly play by the constitutional rules and get very far in implementing their agenda. But the agenda is paramount, so they are willing to break the rules of fair and open debate in order to get what they want. Here are the usual tactics, straight out of the liberal play book.

*Hide your true intention. You know the majority won't like what you really want to do, so conceal the truth, and lie if you have to. Sponsors of the income tax about 90 years ago (via the 16th Amendment to the Constitution), for instance, assured everyone that the rates would never go above 2-3%. In fact, in 1913 only the richest 1% of the population had to pay at all, and then only about 1% of net income, but within a few decades, the maximum rate soared to 91%.

*Image is more important than substance. Something just has to look or sound good, it doesn't have to be good. If some measure like a tax increase is unpopular, try to convince them it's vitally important, like Senator Jim Sasser proclaiming in his thick accent that each and every tax increase was essential for "dafisut (deficit) reduction" (as if reducing spending wasn't even an option).

*Tell people what they want to hear. A good example here occurred when President Clinton decided to attack Yugoslavia to get rid of Slobodan Milosevic and promised that our troops would be out within a year. Everyone, left and right alike, knew it was impossible, but everyone played along, because they genuinely wanted it to be true.

*When in doubt, shout. When you sense you are losing an argument due to faulty logic or lack of facts, turn to emotion and volume to confuse and disorient your opponent. A conservative will generally remain a gentleman and not yell back, leaving his only option an apologetic retreat. Who can ever forget the image of President Clinton angrily pointing his finger and exclaiming, "I did not have sex with that woman…Monica Lewinsky!"

*Always go for the jugular. Don't leave your opponent standing, but rather finish him off completely. Make sure he doesn't come back to debate you another day. Resort to personal attacks when you don't get your way, and keep hammering them home until your opponent gives up. A good example of this was the activist actress Janeane Garofalo, who stated, "What you have now…is people that are closet racists, misogynists, homophobes, and people who love . . . the politics of exclusion identifying as conservative."

*Fool all of the people some of the time, and fool some all of the time. The more audacious the lie, the more effective. If something is just a little off fact and people realize it, they'll call you on it. But if something is completely off the wall and yet you keep insisting it is true, people begin to doubt their own perceptions. Quote made-up statistics, because people tend to believe statistics are scientific and must be real. Remember the claims that the Lewinsky problem was due to a "vast, right wing conspiracy"? Oh, so it had nothing to do with Bill's zipper problems, but a secret cabal of evil right-wingers had plotted with Monica to slip her into the White House and have her lie about an innocent president? Yeah…that's the ticket!

THE RIGHT: Leftists always have to cover their tracks and work at establishing and maintaining a false image. Whereas the Left worries that the public might learn the truth, conservatives worry that they won't.

To conservatives, politics is not a game to be exploited for personal gain so that they can win power and then abuse it. Rather, to conservatives, politics is the flawed but only governmental system we have within which we can hope to achieve good and meaningful societal goals. And you can't achieve noble ends through ignoble means. You can't achieve virginity by having illicit sex, can't enhance health by abusing drugs, and you can't reach truth, justice, and the American way by lying, trickery and demagoguery. In such cases, the means become the ends, a sordid, greasy mess that barely resembles democracy at all.

It is easy to lie, cheat, and con people, but can be difficult honestly to lead them in the right way. But the right way is the only way we can achieve valuable, lasting goals. The Left doesn't seem to care that their political prescriptions don't work but rather make things worse. To them, all that counts is looking good…even if bad results. But conservatives are just the opposite. When they see things turning south they look for honest answers which will help things really get better, whether readily palatable and easy to sell or not.

No, conservatives recognize that they aren't saints or morally perfect. But there is a huge difference between struggling to do the right thing while occasionally falling short and staying up awake nights conniving new ways to trick people.

For example, leftists see the poor and think how they can exploit this subgroup to win more power for themselves. So they create huge new government bureaucracies to provide jobs for more leftists, tax the populace heavily, and foster give-away programs which only make the problems related to poverty immeasurably worse in the long run. For example, Johnson's "War on Poverty" from the 1960's on cost trillions and, by subsidizing broken homes, illegitimacy, and general laziness, helped produce a huge, unproductive, and often criminal underclass.

Conservatives see the poor and think how the problem can actually be remedied, even if the solution will be difficult and meet resistance. They wanted to reform welfare, for example, by requiring recipients to seek work and encouraging the acquisition of skills and creation of stable families. The conservative Welfare Reform Act of 1996, enacted over hysterical left-wing opposition and demagoguery, actually helped stabilize families, get more people back to work, and reduced associated social pathologies. All this, and it saved money to boot!

PORNOGRAPHY

THE LEFT: The First Amendment gives all Americans the absolute right to freedom of expression in all things sexual. Therefore, the Left believes that everyone has the right to read magazines with nude pictures, watch sexually explicit movies and TV, attend nude shows and performances of all types, etc. Everyone has the right to be nude and to see nudity, to be sexually active and to observe sexual activity. It is a good thing when college coeds put videocameras into their dorm rooms and broadcast live over the internet all their activities, including dressing, undressing, and sexual behavior.

Only blue-nose, prudish conservatives are so uptight as not to realize the beauty and value of all that they denigrate by calling it pornography. The very word pornography is offensive, because it implies that there is something wrong with such material. To the contrary, the Left believes that enjoying sexual literature and images is a positively good thing. Sexually inhibited people are frustrated and repressed and tend to get irrational or violent. Allowing free expression is a safety valve that leads to greater mental and emotional health. There would be a lot less violence and insanity in society if there were more sex. Even professional psychiatrists and psychologists would agree. Didn't Sigmund Freud's disciple, Wilhelm Reich, teach that sexual repression led to fascism, but that communism could open up a glorious new era of free sexuality and a freer society? Instead of calling it "pornography" we should call such material and activities "free sexual expression."

So-called pornographers such as Larry Flynt, the publisher of the ultra-sexually-explicit magazine HUSTLER, are actually constitutional heroes, in the eyes of the Left. Flynt is on the cutting edge of defending the First Amendment, ensuring that all Americans can rest freer in the knowledge that their rights to free speech and expression are intact. The movie THE PEOPLE VS LARRY FLYNT won awards for making that case.

The Left thinks it is way past time for antiquated blue laws to be expunged from the books. No more zoning laws to keep porno shops a minimum distance from schools or churches. No more FCC

(Federal Communications Commission) restrictions on TV content, no limits on what sex magazines and books can publish, and finally we can get rid of those "cutesy-poo" cutaways from bedroom scenes in movies. Instead, let it just all hang out, like Janet Jackson at the Superbowl halftime show in 2004. Quit hassling Broadway, other stage shows, and theatrical performances. Quit censoring writers, photographers, and other artists. Don't limit the human mind, man! Make love, not war!

Liberate sex and we'll liberate society!

THE RIGHT: As usual, the Left has it completely, hopelessly backwards. They are just plain wrong in nearly every respect.

First of all, religious Judeo-Christian conservatives generally have not an inhibited, repressed view of sex as something dirty or nasty, but rather a very enlightened view of it as something special and exalted. They believe that human sexuality is a beautiful treasure created and bestowed by God. It can only be enjoyed properly and to the fullest, however, when in a loving and committed heterosexual relationship known as marriage (see **SEXUALITY** below). Sexuality is too beautiful and important to trivialize or tarnish it with pornography. It is not sex, per se, that is bad, but rather the sordid profaning of sex. Surveys of thousands of couples reveal that those who share this view are not inhibited at all, but rather enjoy sex more than the so-called "liberated" ones.

Imagine this metaphor. You can go to the Louvre Museum in Paris and see such beautiful paintings as the Mona Lisa. It is a special, revered painting. We don't want people throwing mud at that painting, or handling it and passing it around, or throwing it on the floor and stepping on it with greasy shoes. The painting is not bad, but the misuse and abuse of the painting would be bad. It is precisely because we do treasure the painting so much that we want to protect it. The left-wing liberals who advocate messing around with the painting are not desiring true liberation at all, but rather degradation, corruption, and the thrill of breaking the rules.

Each person's sexuality is a potential jewel or treasure worth far more than an inanimate painting. And to rob a person of his or her dignity through pornography (whether they are willing or not) is to demean and diminish that person, not liberate him. Wilhelm Reich was a misguided zealot who ended up not liberating anyone else or even himself—he ended up dying in jail. Larry Flynt is pathetic when trying to justify his gross excesses as something noble in terms of defending the Constitution. Such psychological defense mechanisms fool no one except fellow liberals. And not even all of them. Left-wing feminists often agree with conservatives on this one point at least, that pornography demeans women and leads to abuse of them and should thus be opposed.

Fiendish sex criminals of all sorts, when finally apprehended, are commonly found with a large stash of horrendous pornography. Often when imprisoned they'll report how porno first excited them but they then needed to see ever more extreme material to get the same thrill, and finally they needed to practice what they had seen to get a thrill.

Pornography is not a victimless crime, and communities have the right to protect themselves by setting up their own standards, excluding sex shops, porno parlors, X-rated cinemas, and the like. These laws protect society, they don't repress it. The First Amendment says nothing about defending nudity or graphic sex, but rather defends <u>speech</u> itself, the ability to state out loud or publish one's political, religious, or other beliefs. To make a speech or write an article defending porno would be examples of speech protected by the First Amendment. But broadcasting sickeningly explicit and graphic pictures of sex with animals or children or with sado-masochism is not speech at all and it is NOT protected by the real First Amendment of the actual U.S. Constitution. See also **AMENDMENT, FIRST**.

POVERTY

THE LEFT: Poverty results from the greed of the upper classes and from the very nature of the corrupt capitalist system. The monied overlords have a vested interest in suppressing the masses, keeping them poor and under their thumbs. They must have a vast number of powerless drones to do the drudgery jobs like picking grapes, mopping floors, and cleaning toilets. As Karl Marx put it, "Capitalist production, therefore, develops technology, and the combining together of various processes into a social whole, only by sapping the original sources of all wealth - the soil and the labourer." Or as Marshall McLuhan succinctly put it, "Affluence creates poverty."

The Left thinks it is abominable if anyone ever tries to blame poverty on the very people who suffer from it. It's not their fault! They are not responsible! If they are alcoholics or drug addicts and can't keep a job, that is society's fault. If they don't feel like working or have inadequate skills for a higher paying job, that is society's fault, too. So society must provide for all their needs.

The solution is to have everyone share everything equally. As Karl Marx said, "From each according to his abilities; to each according to his needs." That's only fair, right?

Greedy capitalists, however, will never do the right thing unless they are forced. So as the Left sees it, a strong centralized government must step in and compel people to do right by the poor. Government will serve as Robin Hood, taking from "the rich" to give to the poor. The government must ensure complete equity and equality of outcomes in every respect. As President Lyndon Johnson proudly proclaimed in the 1960's, "This administration here and now declares unconditional war on poverty."

The very names of policies reflect the Left's point of view. Having higher and higher tax rates the more money you make is called a "progressive" tax plan. Anything like a flat tax, where everyone pays the same amount or percent (as in a fixed sales tax), is considered "regressive" by definition. And everyone is always for progress, right? So we must have progressive tax laws. That way the rich pay their fair share.

THE RIGHT: Traditional leftist government programs to reduce poverty only make it worse. When you reward people for not working with greater benefits than can be earned in a low-paying job, you create more people who refuse to work. When you create incentives for becoming pregnant out of wedlock, you get more out of wedlock pregnancies. The welfare system prior to its recent reform was a national disgrace that almost single-handedly undermined the African-American community. Whereas 40 years ago, 70% of black families were intact, after decades of the much-vaunted "War on Poverty" 60% of black children are growing up in homes without fathers. Out of wedlock births are three times more common now than then, now up to 70% of all African American births. The message that values and religion and personal responsibility don't count, but that all that matters is government programs, truly sank in...and bore bitter fruit.

Although little helped by leftist welfare programs, poverty actually is not a fixed and permanent state at all. In the old feudal period (and perhaps in other societies today), social class was relatively fixed and permanent. If you were born into a poor family, you would die in a poor family; ditto for someone born wealthy. But fixed social status has never been true in America, and is less so now than in the past. The Federal Reserve Bank of Dallas compared people's socioeconomic standing in 1975 with what it became by 1991, 16 years later. Of those in poverty, those in the bottom fifth of the economic ladder in 1975, only 5% were still there in 1991. The majority made it to the top three-fifths of the ladder, and nearly 29% made it to the top fifth.

Was this progress, this upward mobility, the result of government programs? No, it resulted from people taking responsibility for their lives, getting an education, and working their way up the ladder of success. Much of this improvement over time is just the natural course of the typical lifespan. The average American at age 18 to 22 who is just starting out earns relatively low pay and may struggle financially at first, but over the decades earns promotions, makes more money, and acquires more assets (such as fully paid up cars and a home and hopefully a pension). By the time of retirement that once "poor" boy or girl has commonly become one of the Left's hated "rich."

The solution to poverty, therefore, is not more government welfare giveaway programs, but a system that encourages stable families, personal responsibility, education, hard work, thrift, savings, and investment. Almost any American can work out of the bottom half of wage earners into the top half that way. And plenty will make it to the top fifth or even top 5%. That's precisely how most millionaires are "made," not at all through greed and exploitation as the Left's myths proclaim.

What of those who seemingly can't make it on their own, the physically or mentally handicapped, orphans, destitute widows, etc.? People who are well off definitely should help the less fortunate, but true compassion lies not in government as Robin Hood, but in churches, parachurch organizations, and community/civic groups voluntarily giving of their time and money to help. It is a terrible sin not to help people who desperately need it, but it is also a terrible sin to give a free pass at others' expense to people who could earn a living but refuse to do so. That is how you treat cattle, not human beings.

PRAYER, Public—See **AMENDMENT, FIRST**

RACISM—See **CIVIL RIGHTS**

RELATIVISM

THE LEFT: Everything is relative. There is no such thing as absolute truth. Period.

Einstein's Theory of Relativity proved that long ago. And Heisenberg's Uncertainty Principle proved that we can never be certain about anything, not even the position of a single atom or one of its electrons.

According to the Left, what misguided, primitive, backward, and old-fashioned people (including present-day conservatives) teach as "truth" is just their own biases and their own attempt to gain power over others through political oppression.

Each person constructs his own "truth." It may seem true for him/her/it but it is not objectively true in any everlasting sense. It is only subjectively true, has meaning only between the person's ears, and then perhaps only temporarily. Leftists believe that most people think only once in their lives, but real progressives change their minds on everything as they mature. The older and wiser they get, the more they realize that belief in god is just bunk, rules of sexual morality are written by those with sex partners to keep those without them from having any fun, patriotism and national fervor are just jingoistic projections of infantile ego defense mechanisms, etc.

The Left thinks that conservatives, particularly the religious right wing, who believe in absolute truth are not merely fools, they are blindly dangerous. They must be shunned, marginalized, and opposed at every opportunity before their toxic ideas can poison society any further. They cannot be allowed to impose their vision on others; everyone must be given absolute autonomy and freedom to develop their own belief system and behave accordingly.

The prime function of the educational system, therefore, is to deconstruct all the conventional idiocies that youth have learned at home, in the community, or at church, and convince them that everything is relative. This is particularly important at the college/ university level, because people there will be tomorrow's leaders. Further, youth at that age are already generally questioning the world and what they have been taught about it, so the Left will just encourage that natural process. That is the age when people commonly want to experiment, as with sex and drugs, so it is easy for leftists to convince such youth of the very thing they already want to believe, namely that rules and morality are just political repression and that true liberation and fulfillment lie in "letting it all hang out."

The Left's advice to youth: Forget about objective reality and you can have a lot more fun!

THE RIGHT: It is obvious to anyone with common sense that there is objective reality and absolute truth. People may quibble about some of the lesser details, but the broad outlines are pretty clear.

One of the most obvious examples is the law of gravity. This writer has heard leftists actually argue with a straight face that "anything you believe is true for you," and then when challenged with "so if someone believed they could fly on their own power and jumped off a roof, they could?" actually maintain, "yes, that's right." When this writer challenged them to go try it, they demurred, saying, "that's right if you believe it, but I don't believe it so it wouldn't work for me." Has it ever worked for anyone? How can people so book smart be so unwise about real life? Leftists like this actually are "jumping off the roof" (metaphorically speaking) in so many areas of their lives, in terms of other risky behaviors such as dangerous drugs and sexual perversions. And believing it is okay does not protect them from getting AIDS, or getting brain damage, or ruining society, or dying young and facing their Maker with a seared conscience.

Rather than trying to deconstruct reality and build a fantasy world in which to live, wouldn't it be better to learn about what reality really is and then live accordingly? Think of the entire history of real science and medicine and how advances in discovering and applying absolute truth have made life so much safer and more comfortable in so many ways. But one of many possible examples—early cities centuries ago lacked proper sanitation, no one realized how bacteria and viruses could cause disease, and epidemics could spread unchecked. Bubonic plague, for instance, ravaged Europe repeatedly. No matter what you believed about plague causes, if infected fleas from rats bit you, you would be infected with plague bacteria. Once medical science discovered the truth which had been there all along but went unrecognized for eons, experts could objectively develop strategies to prevent plague.

To say there is such a thing as absolute truth is not to deny that some things are relative, of course. I like shrimp and you like steak. My favorite color is blue; yours is red. So what? Personal preferences may well be relative, but that does not mean that all of reality is. Einstein's Theory of Relativity dealt with space, time, and matter, and he never claimed it had any bearing on religion and morality.

Cultural anthropologists love to operate with the notion that if any culture, anywhere, any time in history "naturally" developed a particular belief or custom (e.g., incest, polygamy, cannibalism), then it must thereby be valid. But not only can individual humans make mistakes, so can human groupings known as societies or cultures. A culture less in tune with objective reality will do less well than one more in tune.

A strange paradox, isn't it, when the most vociferous believers in relativism insist with absolute certainty, with firm conviction in this one—and only one—eternally objective truth: that everything is relative? And isn't it likewise amazing that leftists who insist that every culture is valid and that whatever you believe is true for you have one culture and one belief system—and only one—that they can't stand even to hear about, that makes them quiver in their boots and turn red with rage: namely the Judeo-Christian culture? From whence this implacable hostility towards conservatism generally and Christianity specifically if everything is equally true?

RELIGION, Freedom of—See **AMENDMENT, FIRST**

SEXISM—See **FEMINISM**

SEXUALITY

THE LEFT: As Sigmund Freud explained it, the human being is sexually oriented throughout life, from infancy till death. Sexual desires may change over time, the amount of libido may wax and wane, the principal object of pleasure may experience transformation, but it is all about sex in the broadest sense. The infant knows nothing of genital intercourse, yet is still capable of an embryonic form of sexual pleasure and desire.

If sex is so important throughout life, and if repressing the impulse is bad for one's mental health (see **PORNOGRAPHY** section above), then the Left believes in absolutely free and unfettered sexual expression. Do anything you want with anyone you want as often as you want. In such liberation you can find fulfillment. The only restrictions worth considering relate to mutual consent—you shouldn't hurt anyone else in pursuing your own desires, unless, of course, they want you to (i.e., sado-masochism).

In other words, there is no such thing as perversion or abnormality in sexual expression. Everything goes—everything— provided mutual consent is involved. Society has no business inflicting meaningless bourgeois moral codes on people or restricting them with any kind of law. As the HUMANIST MANIFESTO II (1973) puts it:

"...neither do we wish to prohibit, by law or social sanction, sexual behavior between consenting adults. The many varieties of sexual exploration should not in themselves be considered "evil." Without countenancing mindless permissiveness or unbridled promiscuity, a civilized society should be a tolerant one. Short of harming others or compelling them to do likewise, individuals should be permitted to express their sexual proclivities and pursue their life-styles as they desire."

Many leftists go much farther than saying anything goes just for "consenting adults," and want to eliminate the concept of age of consent. Teens and preteens experimenting with bisexuality? No problem; in fact, it is absolutely normal and healthy. How about the North American Man Boy Love Association (NAMBLA), which openly advocates homosexual contact between grown men and young boys? Don't be a prude, man! Incest? Even the American Psychological Association recently came out in support of it if the partners consented (and then modified their public statements after a firestorm of protest). How about bestiality and necrophilia? Why not? It's only natural and normal if that's what they want. Don't be a stick in the mud, claims the Left, everything goes.

THE RIGHT: The human sexual impulse is indeed very strong, and people do very much desire sexual fulfillment, but true fulfillment can only be found when sexuality is sought within certain protective boundaries. The boundaries—moral laws—are not in place to repress or hurt people, but rather to protect them and maximize their chances for genuine fulfillment.

Try this metaphor: Which of the following is more desirable? (A) Having a choice and delectable banquet where every dish has been painstakingly prepared according to your specifications. There's been waiting involved, but now you are all dressed up and eager for this magnificent feast in this glorious banquet hall. There is romance and everything seems magical as you and your devoted partner sit down to enjoy yourselves. (B) You root about in a pig sty like a common beast, indiscriminately devouring everything in your path, no matter how unsavory, yet never become satisfied. You keep hoping to find a truffle, but encounter grubs and centipedes instead.

How does the moral code protect you? Many leftists (as well as common lechers) believe in "love 'em and leave 'em. No commitments—that's for suckers." That may seem to work for the one making the decision to leave, but how about the person feeling abandoned? The Sexual Revolution since the 1960's has left untold heartbreak in its wake. People who wanted more lasting relationships suddenly found themselves losing everything.

Sex without love may be physically gratifying to an extent but it leaves out the richest dimensions of the experience. It's like watching a color TV with the sound and color off and the tuning mixed up. Yes, you have some grasp of what is going on, but you don't experience it to its fullest.

How does the moral code protect you? Ask the compulsive homosexual man who's had hundreds or even thousands of partners and is now dying of AIDS at age 35. Ask the sexually active teen girl who has had so many STDs (Sexually Transmitted Diseases) by the time she is 20 that she is now permanently sterile and can never have a baby. Ask the kids who have never known their father because their mother brings home a different man every week or so.

And it is not just the individuals who are suffering. The whole society suffers when marriage breaks down as an institution. The family is the foundation of a stable and happy society, and the more broken families the more the whole society struggles and groans. The Right doesn't want laws and government policies that inhibit or repress people, but which provide a stable and harmonious setting in which people can most likely find happiness. Conservatives like school programs which emphasize abstinence before marriage rather than condom giveaways (the condom is not the great and perfect prevent-all as the Left pretends). They want more welfare programs that encourage marriage rather than single parenthood. They are not trying to force people to behave in certain ways, but rather to encourage them.

SOCIALISM

THE LEFT: Socialism is the path to utopia. Inequality breeds misery, and if people are left to their own devices, they will produce inequality. Some people will be bigger or stronger or brighter; they will work harder, scrimp and save; they will end up with more money and goods than others. This is unfair.

The solution is for the government to own everything, for the government to control everything, for the government to manage and run everything. Only the elite of society, who are naturally attracted to working in such government, have the wisdom to centrally plan and organize everything in the best way to ensure equality. They will control the means of production and the means of distribution of what is produced.

Cuba, for example, is a worker's paradise, at least according to the Left. The government tells people what to do and when to do it. Castro's government controls all the resources of the country, including people, property, equipment, and finances. They ensure that everyone has affordable food and free medical care. It is utopia.

Backwards, reactionary democracies like America still cling to the myths of capitalism, freedom, and individuality. It would be difficult to impose socialism all at once on America, so the Left has busily been implementing it gradually over the past several decades, patiently—ever so patiently—making one step at a time.

Take Hillary Clinton, for instance. Early in the Clinton's co-presidency, she developed what was intended to be the most significant socialist step ever to be taken in one jump by America—socialized medicine. But the reactionary greedy conservatives blocked her plan, so the Left had to return to the slower process of incremental changes towards socialized medicine, things like expanding medicare, adding drug benefits, and enforcing universal health insurance. The more control the government gets over everything, the better.

Socialism is a temporary phase on the road to complete communism. In the socialist stage we still need a strong central government to control everything. But as we reach the final stage of human evolution towards communism, a totally class-less society, a new human being will emerge, people will just naturally cooperate and the government will simply wither away, and we will have heaven on earth.

We will also finally have peace on earth, that is, once the right wing is eliminated, re-educated, or at least sufficiently marginalized as to have no power. As Karl Marx famously said, "The meaning of peace is the absence of opposition to socialism. " So the sooner we get those pesky conservatives out of the way, the sooner we'll have peace.

THE RIGHT: Socialism is fool's gold. It may glimmer in the eyes of true believers, but it is utterly worthless. It is worse than worthless; it is counterproductive and produces the exact opposite of what it is supposed to do.

No single body, government or otherwise, can efficiently plan everything. Any person who has had even the briefest acquaintance with any bureaucracy knows how inefficient it can be. You have to submit and resubmit paperwork, you have to take a number and wait in long lines, and often you are confronted with a disinterested bureaucrat. You may have to reapply or appeal or come back later if you don't get what you are entitled to. Not by a long shot are all "public servants" uncaring, but there are enough who are that even something as simple as getting a passport or a drivers' license can sometimes be an upsetting hassle.

It is not centralized control that guarantees efficiency and plenty, but rather freedom, the kind of individual, personal freedom that is only found in democracies, particularly constitutional republics. A million people working towards the betterment of themselves, their families, and their communities with the freedom to respond immediately to the constantly changing economic, environmental, market supply/demand, and other factors around them produce a dynamic, vibrant efficiency unmatched by the most brilliant cabal of central controllers imaginable.

Socialism produces gross inefficiency with a ponderous and inadequate response to changes in the economy, the environment, or other world conditions. Socialism produces not plenty but scarcity for everyone. It is one thing to have "free health care" on paper, and quite another to find that free actually means "scarce" and substandard and requiring a long, long wait and maybe you won't get the life-saving care you need at all before it is too late.

Socialism and communism don't lead to a new and improved evolutionary version of man, because human nature cannot be changed by governmental structures of any sort. So to attain and maintain control, such governments inevitably turn to tyranny, cruelty, and mass murder to force their dictates on an unwilling populace.

Even in Hillary's famed health care plan could be found the seeds of tyranny. The most odious aspect of the plan to freedom-loving people was all the legal restrictions backed up by severe penalties like fines and even jail for not going along with every jot and tittle of the system. If you simply went to your own personal physician like in the good old days you could be considered an outlaw and punished!

Cuba's "worker's paradise" is a hell hole that people will risk their very lives to get away from. The Soviet Union, Red China, and Cambodia with their horrendous population dislocations and death camps were the logical and inevitable result of socialist/communist policies. Even countries that dabble in socialism by the slow and non-violent approach, as in much of Europe, find that the cost is too high and they don't have a money tree in the backyard to fund it.

TAXATION

THE LEFT: Taxation is good. In fact, the more taxation the better. In a greedy capitalistic society such as America, the Left can't simply seize all private property like it did in the Soviet Union and Red China…at least not yet. So taxation remains the only legal and socially acceptable way to redistribute income, to seize from "the rich" what is not rightfully theirs in any case, but should belong to all the people, and then to give it away to the underclass.

The more the Left taxes, the more money it has to give away to buy votes, the more power it gains, the more it can tax. This happy circle left liberals in charge of the Congressional purse strings for some 40 years, until 1994.

The power to tax is also the power to intimidate and destroy one's enemies. Therefore, when the Left is in charge it wants a strong Internal Revenue Service with as many police powers as possible. It can then "sic" the IRS on its political enemies, particularly the religious right. Even when the IRS has no legitimate case, it can hound and harass religious right-wing organizations that dare speak out on political issues and force them to endlessly tie up their money and time defending themselves. The Right has no right to speak out, so if the CHRISTIAN COALITION, the RUTHERFORD INSTITUTE or other conservative groups constantly must spend time meeting IRS demands for ever more records, they can be effectively silenced for a time, or at least stifled.

Taxation must be progressive, meaning that people who make more must not merely pay more total dollars, but must pay at a higher rate. Low-income earners pay no income tax and, in fact, get a bonus back in the form of earned income tax credit. Middle class earners should pay at a fairly low rate, perhaps 14% of their income over a certain minimum. But "the rich" should be soaked. In the Left's taxation heyday (before Kennedy's 1963 income tax cut), the upper rate was 91%. (That would apply not on all income, but only that above a certain amount.) The ultimate leftist goal is to replicate what some European socialist countries have done and confiscate 100% of income at the highest levels, above a certain minimum to live on.

Multiple taxation and hidden taxes are the best way to pluck all the feathers off the goose that lays the golden egg without actually killing it. So the Left wants not only high income tax rates, but a variety of taxes to be as high as possible. The "rich" man who just paid 70% of his income in federal income tax (prior to Reagan's reduction of the maximum rate to 50% and then 28%) then has to pay these other taxes out of the remainder—state income tax, local income tax, property tax, sales tax, excise tax, capital gains tax, special "luxury" taxes, so-called "sin" taxes (on alcohol and tobacco), gift taxes, value added tax (VAT), and ultimately inheritance taxes. That's the way to humble the greedy, selfish rich and bring them back down to the level of the common man where they belong.

THE RIGHT: A certain amount of taxation is necessary to fund the constitutionally specified functions of government, such as to "provide for the common defense and general welfare" (Article I, Section 8 of the U.S. Constitution). But our forefathers in the Colonial period revolted from England largely because of excessive taxes and "taxation without representation." When leftists are in charge, taxation even with representation isn't very palatable either. To leftists who believe in total socialism, all the money in the country belongs ultimately to the government and they want total control over all of it, one way or another.

Tax cuts to a leftist are like castrating his source of power and respect. He will fight them with all the savage rhetoric and dirty tricks at his command. The mere mention of a proposed tax cut is like waving a cross before the Christophobic draculas of the ACLU—they recoil in horror and outrage. It is a knee-jerk response, an ingrained reflex, unthinking and irrational.

Watch a conservative propose a tax cut and you won't have to take another step before leftists are denouncing it as a "giveaway to the rich." When liberals talk like that they forget their strategy is incremental imposition of socialism and betray their true belief that this already is a socialist country where the government owns everything. (See **SOCIALISM**).

Taxes should be kept as low as reasonably possible so that the people who actually earn the money can keep a reasonable amount. The paradox is that when tax rates are cut, total tax revenues often rise as a direct result. The opposite is also true. One of the Clinton debacles was increasing the tax on luxury yachts. The thinking was, if last year the rich spent $310 million on yachts and other luxury items, then a 10% luxury tax this year will produce $31 million more for the Treasury. But increasing the rate led to a reduction in total tax revenues, because people were unwilling to be gouged and thus bought fewer yachts. Not only did the Treasury lose money, but the drop in sales threatened to destroy an industry, wiping out hundreds, perhaps thousands of yacht-building jobs. Conversely, when tax rates are lowered, people have more money to spend and invest, thus creating more economic activity, which leads to more total taxes. The Left pretends to be blind to this fact only because they want the power to control and, if necessary, destroy, no matter what the cost.

A flat tax system, in which low income earners pay nothing and everyone who earns above a certain amount pays the same rate is the way to go. Many ordinary people take a perverse delight in seeing liberals "stick it" to "the rich." They have in mind spoiled moguls who inherited everything and produce nothing themselves. But most millionaires maintain an ordinary standard of living and have attained wealth because they have taken economic risks and worked hard, scrimped, saved, and invested. They have not stolen money from the poor. They have contributed to society and the economy by inventing, developing, or producing new goods and services. And what leftists call "the rich" in terms of income levels is not just millionaires but upper middle class incomes which will be attained by most professionals and other hard-working people at some point in their lives. They already pay more than their fair share in taxes and contributions to society. When leftists say "the rich should pay their fair share" they really mean, "screw the indus-trious and drag them down to the level of the non-productive."

TERRORISM

THE LEFT: Terrorism is the natural response of a people who feel oppressed and downtrodden, and no country has done more oppressing than America, and therefore America richly deserves to be the target of terrorism.

In addition to gloating that America has finally had some comeuppance as the recipient of terrorism, it is important to the Left to lecture Americans on how terrorism is their fault and how only through self-humiliation, propitiation for past sins, and pacifism can they remedy the situation.

First, self-humiliation. The Left believes America must acknowledge its culpability in creating around the world the conditions that lead to terrorism as a natural response. Admitting the blame and meekly accepting one's punishment are the only satisfactory signs of repentance.

Second, America must atone for the sins of the past. Whereas before it exploited the Third World for its natural resources like oil, it must now cease to attain a higher standard of living and seek a more simple, natural lifestyle which does not require the rape of the Third World. Americans can start by banning SUVs, driving less, using less energy of all types, eating a simpler diet (plants vs animal foods), and, in general, trying to live like Third Worlders. As Al Gore states in his book EARTH IN THE BALANCE, automobiles are "posing a mortal threat to the security of every nation that is more deadly than that of any military enemy we are ever again likely to confront." And the Kyoto protocol, if ever ratified, would require reductions in the emission of so-called greenhouse gases in developed countries, which would naturally require the use of less energy, which would lead directly to a contraction in the economy, the loss of jobs, and a lowered standard of living.

Finally, and most important, the Left is convinced that America must resort to total pacifism to prove their intentions are honorable. Fighting back in any form will simply exacerbate the cycle of violence. The very idea of going to war over terrorism is a hideous monstrosity, a relic of unbridled pride and jingoism. Nothing about

America is worth fighting for; the sooner we give up everything that is distinctively American, the better. If we can show the Third World that, as good multiculturalists, we abhor our own culture and instead look up to them as standards of virtue, then they will have no need to attack us, and we will achieve peace. We needn't fight our enemies if we can join them. "The world will be as one" to quote the immortal John Lennon.

THE RIGHT: One thing the Left can never seem to understand is that there is evil in the world, and some people deliberately choose evil. Osama bin Laden was not poor and downtrodden, but wealthy, someone who made millions of dollars off the West. The Left's analysis of the international terrorism situation is flawed in every respect because they are starting from false premises and proceeding from there to ridiculous conclusions. If your whole belief system is based on falsehoods, you will come up with some screwy ideas. Your policy prescriptions will be the opposite of what is really needed. Claiming to be wise, sensitive, and tolerant does not make it so. If your ideas are wrong, no matter how sincerely you believe in them, they won't help. They will only make things worse!

Look at the Clinton administration, for example. The Left considers those co-presidents as the most brilliant international strategists in a long time, but what did they do about terrorism? Mostly bluster and half-hearted attempts to smack down tyrants, with military retreat at the first sign of difficulty. For instance, when Islamic terrorists first tried to destroy the New York World Trade Center towers in 1993, it was treated as a mere law enforcement issue. The perpretrators' colleagues in terror simply came at us again. When we tried to take out the warlord Aideed in Somalia, the Islamic terrorists engineered a trap and near massacre of our military units involved, so Bill ordered the rest out. When Sudan allegedly offered to give him Osama bin Laden on a silver platter, Bill declined. He was willing to take symbolic action after our ships and embassies were attacked, things like firing cruise missiles into the desert, but nothing definitive.

Showing weakness and lack of resolve in the face of evil did not turn our enemies into friends, but rather emboldened them to hit us more and harder, culminating in 9/11. If Gore had been president then, one speculation is that his first "solution" would have been to "open a dialogue" with Islamofascist terrorists, something on an international scale akin to the Clinton proposal to prevent crime through "midnight basketball" leagues. Just roll over like a dog and expose your vulnerable underbelly, and the attacker will respect your helplessness and make friends.

President Bush, on the other hand, analyzed the situation flaw-lessly and took exactly the right action. Put a stop to random, indis-criminate, and obscene violence against innocents through targeted, measured violence against specific perpetrators. Bush rolled back tyranny in Afghanistan and Iraq, much to the Left's shock and dismay. (Most of the hard Left preferred Saddam Hussein to President Bush, though it is inconceivable that anyone could possi-bly prefer a man who fed his enemies live into shredding machines). When Hussein was finally caught cowering in a "spider hole" those indelible images in the news made tyrants all over the world abruptly think twice. All of a sudden dictators like Khaddafy of Libya were willing to give up programs of mass destruction and freely allow U.S. inspection within their borders. They didn't want to be next!

See also **AMERICA**, **ISRAEL**, and **MILITARY**.

TOLERANCE—See **POLITICAL CORRECTNESS**

UNITED NATIONS (U.N.)

THE LEFT: The United Nations (UN) is far, far more important than America. The only possible way to think about America is as a passing phase. Really, it is completely out of date to think about separate nations at all. Breaking down national boundaries, national identities, and national militaries is the only way to move toward global unity and peace at last, according to the Left.

The European countries have the right idea except they are moving too slowly. Less and less do people think of France and Germany and Italy as separate countries. The European Common Market began to bring them together. They stopped having border control, they have moved to a common currency (the euro), and cultural barriers are at last beginning to fall. And look at the wonderful result! What used to be distinct and separate countries, which led to centuries of warfare and bloodshed, now are more like cooperative states in a single country. A hundred years ago, peace in Europe seemed an impossible dream, but now it has been achieved through unity!

That's the Left's model for the future: we need to bring ALL countries together, to dispense with ALL separate national identities, governments, and currencies, etc. The UN is a great step in the right direction, but it has historically been too weak, with the large countries like America and the former Soviet Union having too much power relative to the smaller Third World Nations. But as true, blue multiculturalists, the Left denigrates America and the West generally and puts the tiny or primitive and emerging Third World countries on a pedestal. THEY have much to teach the rest of us, so America should surrender its sovereignty and submit to THEIR leadership for a change. That means no unilateral action of any kind, specifically, military adventurism to implement regime change in Afghanistan and Iraq, and so on.

The planet needs ONE world government, ONE currency, ONE court system, and ONE military. That is all. That is the roadmap for permanent global peace. As the HUMANIST MANIFESTO II (1973) puts it in its twelfth proposition, "We deplore the division of humankind on nationalistic grounds. We have reached a turning point in human history where the best option is to transcend the limits of national sovereignty and to move toward the building of a world community in which all sectors of the human family can participate. Thus we look to the development of a system of world law and a world order based upon transnational federal government.... Human progress, however, can no longer be achieved by focusing on one section of the world, Western or Eastern, developed or underdeveloped. For the first time in human history, no part of humankind can be isolated from any other. Each person's future is in some way linked to all. We thus reaffirm a commitment to the building of world community, at the same time recognizing that this commits us to some hard choices."

THE RIGHT: The idea of peace through unity sounds wonderful, but we must consider not just an idealistic vision but how it would be implemented. In terms of unity and peace, Europe has been doing pretty well recently. Only about a half century ago, Nazi Germany sought to conquer Europe and slaughtered millions of people. Now you can drive from Germany to France without even encountering a border guard; it is the same as driving from New Hampshire to Vermont. This unity was not imposed from without, however, but was achieved by free nations freely developing and recognizing their unity of purpose.

If the pilot, co-pilot, and navigator of a plane all agree on where they are going, then they can naturally cooperate and work together and have a smooth flight. That's what is happening in Europe. But if the pilot wants to go from Dulles airport to L.A. and a terrorist onboard takes over the plane and wants to fly it into the Pentagon, there is no unity of purpose, and only disaster, tragedy and suffering result. Cooperation by the flight crew in such a case is lunacy and means total destruction.

Unfortunately, the UN and all the Left's mighty hopes for

global unity resemble more the latter model. If every country and every person meant well, that would be fantastic. But it is not realistic and will never happen. There are enemies of freedom in the world who want not to cooperate, but to destroy our way of life; not to achieve peace, but to eliminate us; not to help, but to conquer and hurt in any way possible. America must never voluntarily surrender sovereignty to the U.N. or any other such body, must never let down her guard and trust solely in the well-wishes of Third World or other countries, must never stop...being America!

Note the Humanist Manifesto II's closing words in the quote above—"building of world community...commits us to some hard choices." It has been prophesied in Scripture that the Left's goal of a one-world government will eventually be largely achieved, but at a terrible cost and with not peace but bloodshed resulting, not freedom, but the most horrible tyranny ever known. When there is a one-world monetary system, each legally recognized citizen will have to submit to the global tyranny and accept a true Master Credit card-like number, but the number will be implanted on the skin of the right hand or forehead. Without that number, without becoming a slave in the global system, one will not be able to pay rent, to buy and sell in the marketplace, to go to the grocery and legally obtain food. Anyone refusing on religious grounds (for Scripture gives a very stern warning NOT to accept the one-worlders' number) will be persecuted, imprisoned, and killed.

The Humanists' "hard choices" will mean forcing people to do what the Left wants and slaughtering those who stand in the way.

WAR—See **MILITARY**

WELFARE—See **POVERTY**